T0299565

the book
your dog
wishes
you would
read

the book
your dog
wishes
you would
read

LOUISE
GLAZEBROOK

First published in Great Britain in 2021 by Orion Spring
an imprint of The Orion Publishing Group Ltd
Carmelite House, 50 Victoria Embankment
London EC4Y ODZ

An Hachette UK Company

9 10

A CIP catalogue record for this book is
available from the British Library.

ISBN (Hardback) 978 1 3987 0406 0
ISBN (eBook) 978 1 3987 0407 7
ISBN (Audio) 978 1 3987 0408 4

Printed and bound in Great Britain by
Clays Ltd, Elcograf, S.p.A.

www.orionbooks.co.uk

For my husband and my children: never stop believing that you can make a difference, no matter how small that change may be. This book is the proof of that. xx

For Gussy, Cookie Dough, Barnie Boy, Freddy Bear, Pip Squeak and Happy, and every other dog I've ever met, worked and played with.

CONTENTS

Why This Book Is Here

Last summer, I sat on Walberswick beach in Suffolk, on a family holiday with my parents, my sister and her children and my kids. We had lost our darling Fred, a Great Dane, in the April, and so for the first time in the history of my children's lives, we were without a dog. I felt bereft, as both the beach and our entire English seaside holiday were perfect for a dog.

As we sat there together, I noticed a family with a little black Labrador puppy, the breed that my six-year-old son was absolutely desperate for us to get. Watching the family, I had to physically restrain myself from going over to intervene.

It wasn't that they were being cruel, unkind or nasty – it was simply that they didn't understand that the way they were playing and teasing the dog would come back to, literally, bite them on the bum.

The puppy was probably around twelve weeks old. The dad was playing a game of lying on the sand with the puppy and teasing him with his hands, and the kids joined in. Stoking the puppy up, getting him to chase their hands, which inevitably turned into play biting – to which the dad took offence. The pup was told off by both dad and kids. Yet they were the ones who began the game, they were the ones who pushed him, encouraged him to chase their hands and then were annoyed when his excitement bubbled over into biting.

This chubby puppy, full of love and wonder, didn't understand what he was being told off for. So he began to walk away, using the most gentle tactic a dog knows: to disengage. When he tried, though, they wouldn't allow him to walk away. One child grabbed him from behind and brought him back into the group on the sand.

This was just a brief interaction, no more than a few minutes long. But, watching from along the beach, I could see that it taught that young puppy several things that would stick, including:

1. You get shouted at if you play
2. Humans can't be trusted
3. Walking away doesn't work.

That puppy was wonderful. I could have scooped him up in my arms and run off with him into the sunset. All I could think about was how they were creating issues that, in a few months and years, they would need to spend a lot of time and effort and potentially money on changing. Which just seemed ridiculous. These were not mean owners, and they didn't intend to be unkind. They just did not understand that their interactions would create lasting impressions, with consequences for their dog's future behaviour.

I understand that we all make mistakes. It's impossible not to, and it's also one of the ways we learn to do better. Yet we are putting to sleep around 30,000 dogs a year in the UK and around 670,000 in the USA. And as a dog behaviourist it is my experience that these issues more often stem from the behaviour of the owner than that of the dog, who is just being a dog, and needs to be understood like one.

I believe a happier relationship with your dog starts with you, the owner. This is a book to empower you, to help you consider your dog's point of view, to enable you to create a lifelong bond with the amazing animal who shares your life.

When I work with puppies, dogs and rescue dogs, it is my task to help prevent or remedy issues, to help families build a trusting, loving, secure relationship with their new dog. And this is the very reason that this book is here – to help you do the same. To help you not make the innocent mistakes made by those puppy owners on the beach. I believe in setting people and dogs up to succeed, and this is what this book is all about.

You will not find step-by-step guides on how to teach your puppy to sit within these pages. This book is about far more than that. It is about understanding your dog, seeing why certain traits or habits form, and what you can do about them. About how you can learn about the incredibleness of your dog and to enable you to live a more content life together.

Life is never perfect, and I don't promise you the perfect puppy or dog. My method is about moving forward with love and empathy, starting where you are now, and loving your dog in the way they deserve.

I believe this book tells you everything your dog would tell you if it could.

Dogs rule. Let's get to know them better.

L

x

PART ONE

Understanding Your Dog

CHAPTER ONE

Your Dog

I am not a sheepdog trainer, a gun dog person or a canine agility expert. Instead, my work is entirely based around dogs as human companions, as that is all I know and it is all I want. I can't function without a dog in my life; they are my obsession, and my work is fuelled by wanting all dogs to be given the respect and love they deserve. I'm motivated not by achieving 'obedience' or instilling 'commands' but by helping humans and dogs share a happy, fulfilling life together. It is that simple for me and my clients.

I believe that dog ownership is a privilege that we should never take for granted. A dog doesn't exist just to be commanded by us, to live by our rules and to do as we say. It's like any relationship – there needs to be understanding on both sides. Sharing our lives with a dog is an honour, and we should treat our dog with respect and understanding.

At the same time, this book isn't a wishy-washy, let's-just-all-love-each-other-and-hope-for-the-best type of approach. There are tools we can all use to help our dogs and ourselves, and I am excited to share some of these with you in the following pages. You may also have to face your own behaviours in order to help your dog, and yourself.

The common thread of my approach is that I have an honest, caring and kind relationship with every dog I work with. But beyond that I believe that the best approach for a dog is individual – there is no one-size-fits-all approach – which is why so many people are struggling with their dogs. It is also why you won't find some common but complex behavioural issues discussed on these pages, as it's impossible to give tailored advice in a general book – in that case I would always advise working directly with a professional who can get to know your dog as an individual.

We have all fallen into the trap of believing what our friend tells us about how to train a dog, or thinking our new dog will be the same as the one we had as a child. Yet every single dog that enters your life is different. Each has their inbuilt wiring, their personality, their genes, their desires, their challenges and their abilities. I truly think this needs to be kept at the forefront of your mind, for the rest of your life. Understanding your dog as an individual, not just a generic 'dog', will alter the expectations you put on yourself and your dog, which means that you will be much more able to enjoy building the foundations with them.

We live in a world where people want things very fast and immediately, which is why so many people struggle with taking on a dog. A dog doesn't have that sense of urgency about life. It doesn't understand your timetable. It wants to explore, to enjoy the world it lives in, to see the good in everything, and it wants to take its time to learn – and then it finds itself with an owner trying to speed everything up. We want our dog toilet-trained in two weeks, to come back to us every single time at three months old, to never ever put a foot wrong by the time they are six months.

Sometimes I wonder if people are expecting a robot rather than a living creature with its own wants and needs. I often receive emails from people saying something like, 'I pick my puppy up on Saturday and I've taken the next couple of weeks off work to get them used to being left alone and to get on top of the toilet-training.' And I have to reply and say, 'You won't even be touching the sides with that time frame. I would revisit getting a puppy or dog when you have far more time to give, as you will only end up feeling like you are failing and frustrated as you will not be capable of providing the time a puppy needs to thrive.'

Before we go any further, I hope we are working on the basis that you are looking for a companion with its own personality rather than an emotionless robot who obeys every command you utter. I believe you can have a well-behaved dog who is a pleasure to live with, but you can't have an automaton who always does what it's told and adapts itself perfectly to your every demand. My assumption of you as a reader is that you want to share your home life with a four-legged, licking, mischief-making, fun-loving, patience-testing dog, who will live out its life in your care. Way more fun than a robot.

So rather than focus on the essential commands, or behavioural problems that need fixing, I want to start by introducing you to my principles of dog behaviour. Once you understand your dog better, its behaviour becomes less something to be fixed than to be managed with compassion and confidence.

LOUISE GLAZEBROOK

THE SENSORY DOG

Firstly, it is essential to understand your dog as a sensory creature. By which I mean that, just like us, our dogs experience the world with their whole bodies, and all of their senses. My clients often say they wish they knew what their dog was thinking, when a better question might be 'What is my dog smelling, tasting, touching, seeing, hearing?' Their ears, their eyes, their nose and even their fur impact on how each dog views the world around them.

And this can be very breed-specific. For example, an English Bull Terrier has very tight skin; it has a huge, hard head, with its eyes positioned slightly differently from many other head shapes of dogs, to the side rather than facing forward. So the way it walks, the way it experiences the world, the way it reacts to stimuli is going to be really different from a breed like a working Cocker Spaniel. In a working Cocker, breeding has created a dog who cannot switch off, whose nose is constantly absorbing, whose ears are super sound sensitive, making lead work a very tiring and laborious job with this breed.

As sensory beings, all dogs will use their nose, their eyes, their ears, their skin and fur to navigate the world and it is important that we understand the physical and mental differences these sensory abilities create for our individual dogs.

All of a dog's senses need to be engaged, every day, for them to feel fulfilled and content. They need an output or a channel for their ever-sniffing nose, they need to hold and feel different things within their mouth, to be taken on walks that allow them to sniff, to investigate, to run, to play, to experience the natural world properly. Not just walking along a concrete high street where all that exists is litter and noise. It sounds like an obvious statement, but if you understand your dog's sensory needs, in the same way you already understand that a dog needs food, exercise and sleep, it puts a different perspective on their behaviour, whether that is chewing, stopping stock-still on the pavement or sniffing. These senses also greatly impact a dog's ability to regulate its behaviour, affecting how it can (or can't) cope in certain situations.

Smell (olfactory system)

For dogs, their sense of smell is their most important sense, hearing would come after that and then sight. So while we humans encounter the world first with our eyes, dogs encounter it first with their noses. For them, scent is how they build an understanding of their environment. Sniffing is not a nice added extra in your dog's life, it is an absolute necessity. Not allowing your dog to sniff is like you being dragged down the street with a blindfold on – you're not able to fully take in your environment, and it feels bewildering and confusing. Of course you don't always have the time to let your dog engage with every single smell it encounters on a walk, but understanding that stopping to sniff is an essential physical need of your dog, and not something to be discouraged, is key in maintaining a happy pup.

Hearing (auditory system)

The second most important sense for a dog is hearing. A dog's hearing is believed to be able to hear things four times the distance away than a human can detect. Their ability to hear high-pitched noises is incomparable to our own – this means that a noise we barely notice may be distracting or even distressing to our dog. Many breeds are what I call 'noise sensitive', so they seem to respond far more dramatically than some other breeds. My rescue dog Pip has super-sensitive hearing, his ears are constantly moving and sometimes, even when sleeping, will be taking in sounds that are taking place but that I've not even noticed. This is why, with young kids in our house, I have a safe space for him upstairs so that he can shelter from their noise and properly rest. I also find that the noise-sensitive dogs are more nervous, more scared about approaching life in a confident way. I cannot change their noise sensitivity (though some medications can help them live with it if it all becomes too much and really affects their life), but I can look at how to use their other senses to help them regulate, to build their confidence and to help them enjoy the environment around them (you will be able to read more about this in the games and mental stimulation tasks section, later in the book).

Touch (tactile system)

Touch can be a hard sense to gauge, but it is crucial that we try to understand how objects and sensations might feel to our dogs. What feels comfortable and acceptable to one dog might be stressful for another. My English Bulldog used to love rough play; when rubbed down with a towel she bounced at you to give her more. Whereas Pip, our rescue Smooth-coated Collie, is very touch sensitive. It has taken me nearly two years to get him to even consider playing with a tugger toy, as it is just too full on and physical for him. So the way that I use the tugger game with him would be very different from how I use it with, say, a bull breed, which instinctively loves those games. The sense of touch a dog enjoys receiving from humans also differs from dog to dog in terms of what can be tolerated.

Mouth and taste (gustatory system)

Dogs use their mouths to explore objects in much the same way as we might use our hands, so they may pick things up just to work out what they are, rather than because they want to eat them. In addition, mouthing, chewing, licking and sucking can all be sensory regulating for a dog, helping to calm the nervous system. When a dog chews something that you consider precious, it may be doing it to try to de-stress – it certainly isn't trying to annoy you or be destructive for fun.

Sight (visual system)

Vision is of course a sense that dogs use every day, but sight isn't as important to a dog as it is to us because they use their nose and ears so much more than we do. A dog's vision is not as good as ours, which can explain why they can be freaked out by unexpected things like a tarpaulin blowing in the wind, or a suitcase on wheels. Vision is most relevant when we have dogs that are prey motivated or movement motivated, as this can complicate their ability to focus, to listen and to learn. If you have a sight hound or prey-driven dog, you must remember that you cannot simply switch this hunting instinct off. We have bred these dogs to chase for thousands of years, so it's not fair of us to then get annoyed when they run off after a squirrel.

WHAT A DOG NEEDS FROM YOU

Before you even think of getting a dog, you need to consider what every dog needs in order to thrive. For me, these are *needs*, not *nice to haves*, so you really need to consider this and whether you are in a position to be able to fulfil these needs. Really ask yourself if you are ready to provide these for a dog, and whether your lifestyle permits this:

1. A trusting relationship built on love, kindness, patience and understanding. Many new dog owners assume that taking on a dog will 'solve' an already existing relationship issue with another human. It will not. If you are

also looking to bring in a dog on behalf of a child, e.g. a child with special needs, do not be fooled into thinking that just any dog is capable of handling this type of relationship. A dog needs balance itself, and it can't create balance where there is none. I have met many dogs with behavioural issues who are simply mirroring what is going on within the household – splitting time between partners, or reacting to huge explosive arguments. Dogs are emotional beings, and we feed into each other. This is really very important to consider on a basic level but also when deciding on your actual dog and its nature, experience, personality and so forth.

2. Boundaries. These need to be clear and predictable for a dog to feel safe.

3. If you struggle with providing boundaries, it can make life with a dog very hard, as they won't know where they stand or what is expected. Dogs like a black-and-white scenario; they don't like grey, blurred areas that are unclear. I find many breeds really thrive on a routine format. Dogs like the Hungarian Vizsla and the Weimaraner are examples of highly strung, highly driven dogs who need a rigid template to live their lives happily. So compatibility is key when making your selection.

4. Stimulation. Both physical and mental stimulation are as important as each other. You need to consider what stimulation and engagement you are able to provide for a dog and weigh up whether it is enough. Dogs want to play, they want to get out and about, they want to engage, they want to join in, so you need to be

very honest about how you will manage to supply the physical requirements of walking a dog each day, providing exercise off the lead as well as creating playful games, engaging mental stimulation tasks and activities on a daily basis. One client recently said to me, 'You are asking me to put a lot of effort in. When will this be able to lessen on a walk?' If this is your thought process too, I probably wouldn't move forward with taking on a dog. The effort is for life.

5. Consistency. A lack of consistency can make life too unpredictable for a dog. I sometimes meet people who believe they will 'share' the dog with another household. And I have to say, this very rarely works out. Usually it ends up in the dog living in one home and the other person looking after them for holidays or weekends away occasionally. This is because a dog likes to know what is expected of them, where their bed is, where the safe space is, the logistics of the home where they live and so forth. When we start mixing this up too much, we can end up with insecure dogs peeing in their own beds all the time, trying to reassure themselves. We can have confused, frantic behaviour, as they feel uncertain and unsure.

WHAT YOU NEED FROM YOUR DOG

The ideal relationship between a dog and its owner takes account of the needs of both. We should be looking to make sure that any dog and human relationship being entered into is mutually beneficial. This is key to it being successful. I do not believe that any dog is looking to take over your life. They are not seeking dominance. I do not believe that you need to exert some higher status of 'pack leader' in order to be able to live with your future dog. What I do believe in is making sure that you and your dog are well matched.

Are you being selfish in your desire for a dog? I don't mean this unkindly, but it is a question I wish more people would truly sit with and think about, as it could reduce so much heartache. Are you trying to use a dog to 'fix' an area of your life? If so, you need to really consider whether this is a fair expectation of the dog and what you will do and how you will feel when the dog isn't the miracle cure-all you expected it to be.

Are you ready for a commitment that may last for fifteen years or more? If you are ready to take on the responsibility for another living being, and its happiness, then I think you need to be very clear about what is needed on both sides.

I believe that we should be selecting a dog based on their personality, their behaviour traits and their ability to adapt into the life we lead. Instead, what we tend to do – and what I see all the time – is to instead pick a dog based on its looks. The colour of its fur or how great it would look walking on the end of the lead as you waltz down the high street. Your selection process needs to be far more detailed; it needs to be less 'What can I find and pick up within the next couple of weeks?' and more based on months of research, discussion and visiting rescue centres or breeders.

Over the years I've found the Hungarian Vizsla to be one of the most sought after for its ginger velvet beauty, yet many people have zero comprehension of what a full-on, active, challenging breed they actually are.

I have even had people pay me to ask for my tailored advice, to help them select and narrow down some breeds that could work for their lifestyle – and then they go and ignore everything I have said because the image is their overriding element of why they have selected a dog. Take the man who wanted a chilled-out, easy-to-train but not demanding dog who went against all my advice and selected a working Cocker Spaniel from a farm. That dog will not be what he wanted but it was available sooner than any litters of the breeds I'd advised. My view is, better to wait a few months now than regret your decision for the next few years of your life.

WORKING OUT THE RIGHT DOG FOR YOU

Whether you are taking on a puppy or a rescue dog, I urge you to write down answers to the following questions. If there are multiple members of the family, you should all fill out your own and then all sit and compare. Go through it and see where the similarities and differences are, until you can all agree on a set list to use for your search. Most of all, you must be honest. Try to forget any breeds you may like or dislike, and just answer the questions.

1. Write down the five most important qualities of a dog for you: (e.g. affectionate, loving, independent, not needy, super active, etc.)

2. Describe what you envisage doing with this dog of yours: (e.g. snuggling up on the sofa, mountain walks, playing football)

3. Write down five things you dislike about dogs you know or have met: (e.g. barking, not wanting attention, slobber, fur type)

4. What kind of exercise would you like to do with your dog on a daily basis: (e.g. on the school run, pop to the shop, two hours off lead. Remember that exercise you do at the weekend is not 'daily'.)

5. Make a list of the areas you are happy to put work into: (e.g. pulling on the lead, recall, jumping up, aggression, reactivity)

6. Make a list of the areas you are not willing to put time into: (e.g. taking on a dog who needs two hours' walking a day, or a dog who doesn't like children, or a dog that will need bathing daily due to its fur). There should be no judgement here, this is your life too.

7. Coat type and fur – do you care? Shedding, non-shedding? Will the dog need regular trips to the groomer? And if you do care about this, what is the bit you care about? (e.g. making a mess of the sofa, the hoovering-up, the brushing, the feel of it)

8. Note any household restrictions that need to be factored in and cannot be budged on: (e.g. SEN children, other pets, no garden, living on a busy road which would not be good for a sound-sensitive dog)

9. On a daily basis, describe the life you will lead with this new dog: (e.g. going to work on the train, working from home, how many walks per day, where will

it be walked, around lots of people at the studio with you, etc.)

10. How will you factor in entertaining and providing what the dog needs each day? Dogs are not designed to sit at home alone, they are social animals who desire company, interaction and involvement. This is crucial to discuss as a family. Children often say they will take an avid role in caring for the dog, but it rarely happens, so it is up to the adults to discuss the true impact and feasibility on this front.

11. Have you ruled out any allergies? Every dog and its coat differs, as do people's tolerances, so I'd suggest spending time with the very specific breed you are considering. That time should be spent both indoors and outdoors, over at least a couple of hours and over numerous occasions. Even this isn't fail-safe.

Your answers to these questions will be needed later on in the book, so keep them safe.

KEY DOG/PUPPY TIMELINES

I think knowing some key timelines can help you be realistic about the dog or puppy you may be considering taking on, or already have sharing your life. There is no point assuming you can have your puppy fully trained and happy to sleep in a basket next to your desk in a matter of weeks. Be prepared, and you and your pup will both be set up to make this relationship as happy as possible.

How much time should I spend trying to find the right dog?

- To find a puppy or a rescue dog, you should allocate around six months as a minimum – do not rush the process under any circumstances. The work you put in will pay off in the long run.

How long does puppyhood last?

- I usually classify a puppy to be a puppy from birth to approx. twelve–eighteen months. Actually it's more like up to around six to nine months, but I feel like the ten-month mark can be tricky too in terms of puppyhood as this is when breed-specific traits like barking or guarding might emerge. So I'd always consider puppyhood to be a full year plus a bit more – some breeds up to two or three years.
- Puppy to full maturity takes around eighteen months. Unless you have a slow-to-mature breed, such as a Labrador, a Vizsla or a Boxer, and then we are talking more like two to three years!

How long does puppy teething last?

- Teething starts as early as eight weeks for some dogs, and can last for several months. Many believe that teething periods are set in stone for every dog, but they truly are not. They vary and some will be far worse than others. If you took your dog early from the litter e.g. at five to seven weeks, you would notice many more teething problems and some that won't ever be remedied due to that early removal. This is because during that formative time, a well-bred puppy will learn from its mother and littermates about mouthing and bite inhibition – when it is too hard, too much and when to stop.

•

How long does it take to toilet-train a dog?
- Toilet-training can be as quick as two weeks or may take six to seven months to achieve. This will depend on the breed, their breeding, the environment they were raised in, the dog's puppy set-up and more. The Shih Tzu, for example, is easy to toilet-train, as is a Poodle, while you may find it harder if you've taken home a Dachshund. You sometimes find that badly bred dogs from puppy farms may never be fully toilet-trained, as they have been raised in squalor and filth from day one.

How long does it take before a puppy can be left on its own?
- To teach a puppy to be able to be left alone, you should set aside around six months, especially if you are taking on a highly dependent breed like a Cockapoo, Cavapoo or Smooth-coated Dachshund. I do not believe that any dog should be left alone for longer than four hours at a time when they are an adult dog. Being able to leave a dog for a few hours requires training, which I explain in more detail in Chapter Nineteen.

How long does it take before my dog will come back to me when I call?
- Recall training is not something that you simply teach and then move on. During the first ten months, a

pup's recall ability will go well and then slip away. You have to keep going with the training and know that by around two years old it should feel fairly cemented so long as there are no dramatic experiences.

How long will it take for my rescue dog to settle in?

- If you take on a reactive dog, by which I mean a dog who reacts either aggressively or with fear to various things, then depending on the reasons, the experiences, the breed and the set-up you have, it could take months or years for the dog to be calm and settled. For some dogs, it will always be a process of management and there may not be an end in sight for difficult behaviours. There are no magic tools, no quick fixes or magic wands, and it is important to be realistic about this. You may need to alter your life, the way you do things and make huge changes you had never considered before taking on a dog. I have a client who has a third-hand rescue who has to be muzzled in their garden, due to his predatory behaviour and the fact he has killed cats in previous homes.

TRAINING VS BEHAVIOUR

When people arrive at my puppy classes, they often want to tell me how many commands they have already taught their pup. In truth, knowledge of commands tells me very little about the puppy's behaviour. I've seen a dog who belonged to this amazing agility dog trainer – it would leap up on his back and over his head; I could never train a dog to do this (and nor would I have wanted to with my Great Dane). Yet this same man couldn't control his dog off lead and I once saw the dog ignore every word his owner uttered as it ran off down the Marylebone Road in Central London in pursuit of some fun of its own. I am only mentioning this to remind you that commands do not make the dog. Which is more important to you, a dog that can offer you a paw or one who is confident and happy within itself and loves to learn with you?

My dog doesn't know how to pull open a set of drawers, nor will he pick up the newspaper and drop it at my toes, and I'm fine with that. My focus is on his behaviour around my children, whether he will stick close to us in the park, if I can walk him through busy streets, and if he can live happily with us and our other pets.

I sometimes worry that there is a growing trend for dog owners to miss the boat on building relationships, building trust and having fun together in pursuit of having a dog who can roll over or shake hands. Which reminds me, don't ever teach your dog to 'paw' as it will become the most annoying thing you have ever taught them, when they are batting you with a huge furry clawed limb to get you to give them things.

I believe there is a big difference between training and behaviour work. Let me explain. If we take a reactive, aggressive dog who is lunging, barking and reacting to other dogs in the park, a trainer may look at simply stopping the action. That would mean getting rid of the annoying barking, the lunging and the embarrassment the owner is feeling. Instead, a dog behaviourist looks at the reasons behind the actions. For every behaviour there is a reason, an underlying foundation, an issue that the dog is trying to solve themselves. The reactivity with other dogs may be for many reasons: fear, frustration, previous experiences of attacks. Understanding the behaviour is more important than training a dog out of it. Understanding means you begin to work with the behaviour and attempt to resolve it. And if it is not solvable, as some things are not, then it will inform the management and day-to-day life strategies that the dog requires to live happily. So when you are trying to resolve issues, I would always suggest that you stop thinking about your immediate need to stop the behaviour. Instead, think about why the dog is doing it – it will serve you far better.

I also find that clients come to me asking for help training their dog out of a behaviour that can be easily managed instead. I've had clients prepared to spend a lot of money to learn how to stop their dog stealing food from the kitchen table or worktop. Admittedly this is annoying behaviour, but it is easier to manage it than to train a dog out of it. I'd struggle to get my six-year-old daughter to leave a packet of sweets alone if I left the room, so I don't leave them there to tempt her. The same applies to your dog, especially if you have a greedy breed like a Labrador or a Pug. Your dog can't steal an open packet of ham from the worktop if it isn't left there in the first place. Please do not punish your dog for simply doing what comes naturally to it. Set yourself, and your dog, up for success by pre-empting situations that might cause problems. It is management rather than training, and I'm fine with that and so should you be.

CHAPTER TWO

Understanding Breeds and Behaviour

Here's where you need your checklist from the previous chapter. I got you to do that questionnaire first as this is the MOST important part of choosing the right dog. Now it's time to either write down the breeds you like or are drawn to and begin to go through each breed and compare it with your list of requirements for a dog that will suit your set-up. You must exclude the ones who simply do not match up. Do not try to make them match up, I promise that you will make yourself very unhappy in the long run if you do this! And you will end up paying a great deal of money to someone like me, trying to get help to stop your dog doing all the things they were literally bred to do – e.g. trying to stop a Dachshund from barking!

We often delude ourselves in order to justify the selection of a certain breed of dog. These delusions can range from saying we will walk a dog for two and a half hours every day, to convincing ourselves we would love an independent dog just because we like its fox-like appearance. As a species, we humans are incredibly reliant on being drawn to the 'look' of a dog rather than its temperament and really, it is my belief, we should be marrying the two together.

I work with clients to help them figure out the most suitable dog for their life and some of these people seek out my help and then actively choose the exact opposite of what I've suggested. One family spent months working with me. I drove to meet the breeder with them, they asked my advice on which puppy to choose to be the most suitable for them as a family and for their child, who was lacking in confidence. They then chose a totally different dog from the one I put forward, based purely on the fact they preferred the white mark on its chest. And the reason people do this is that they believe that 'their dog' will be different. It's a lovely idea that you as one person have that much ability and control to change something, but it isn't factually true.

If it were that true, it would mean that the breeding of dogs wouldn't matter, however badly it was done; that it would create very little impact on the dog you grow up with. And this just isn't true.

A client just emailed me to say they were struggling with the barking of their fourteen-week-old Dachshund puppy. My response was, 'Yes, you have a Dachshund, they love to bark. They were bred to go down holes, find creatures to kill and bark to alert. We have created this breed and its behaviours.' You can't train a dog out of its breed behaviour and nor should you try.

To give you an idea of how to have a Smooth-coated Dachshund who doesn't bark at everything, you would need to have:
• Found a mother and father of the litter who are not nervous, alert barkers, overexcited or highly anxious.

- The parents to love people and other dogs.
- The breeder to not be encouraging anxious puppies who cannot bear to be apart from the person they live with.
- Selected the exact right personality of a puppy from that litter.
- Made sure that the litter is even, that the temperaments do not vary so enormously that you have to choose either the super-pushy dog or the one who sits in the corner not wanting to be touched by anyone. That isn't a balanced litter. An even litter matters because it will be an indicator of the 'type' of dog you may end up with, so don't ignore the signs that are present.
- Looked at the number of puppies within that litter to see how they handle or don't handle frustration, and what their levels of resilience are like.
- Understood what the mother of the litter has been like in the primary socialisation period. Has she barked at everything? Does she bark at the door? In that case, your fate is set.
- Be absolutely confident that the breeder you are buying from is shaping the puppies in the best way possible – not too much handling but not too little. Who is in the household, what life experiences are they having while with the breeder, are they being allowed to explore or are they being contained and never allowed out of a pen?
- And then we still have all the things you would need to be doing once you have brought that puppy home to ensure it doesn't bark a lot.

The honest reality is that most people find a breeder and tell them they want a certain sex and a certain colour. That is generally the most we can expect of a 'selection process' that certainly will not serve you well in the hunt for the quiet Daxie! Or for any dog for that matter. The selection process for your lifelong canine companion should be based on far, far more than a gender and colour of fur.

I don't mean any of this to demoralise you, but more to serve as an illustration of how much effort needs to be put into the selection of a dog. Understand the characteristics of each breed and you're halfway towards making the right decision.

Every single dog can be an incredible pet, when they are bred well living in the right home, with the right stimulus and the right family. But I can't stress how important it is to do your homework at the beginning. Always remember that breeders are not an independent voice. They are obsessed with the particular breed they work with. You must seek out the voice of people who have no vested interest in your selection. Behaviourists like me see hundreds, if not thousands, of dogs and puppies every day, every week and every year whose owners are asking us to train them out of breed-specific traits. We can't do it, and nor should we.

For example, Belgian Malinois are incredibly beautiful, powerful dogs who are often used by the police service for good reason. Their high drive, intelligence, willingness to learn and desire for a job means that when they are doing those demanding jobs they are incredibly happy and fulfilled. In turn, this also means that taking on one of these dogs as just a pet will not work. They will not have a job, they will not be busy and they will not be content, which will mean huge issues for you as an owner. Do not ignore a breed's needs. It will make your life and the dog's life very unenjoyable.

Please don't kid yourself at the start by saying your dog will be different from all the other dogs of its breed. Look at whether you actively want to deal with the challenges of that breed; and if not, keep looking.

BREED GROUPS

I long ago realised that many people don't know what breed group their dog sits in or why, and that means they are at a huge disadvantage in understanding the common behaviours of dogs like theirs. So instead of simply listing the dogs under each grouping, I'm going to give you some common traits and challenges of these groups – to help you understand the impact of their thousands of years of breeding. These are by no means in depth, but they should highlight the need to investigate further and consider the impact of the traits. I'm not saying I 100 per cent agree with all of the groups or the way they are put together. I actually think they could do with sorting out and reclassifying. But that is a job for another time!

Hound Group

These dogs are bred to use their noses and/or eyes to track, chase and alert to prey. With this in mind, it is important to remember that these dogs are not designed to work alongside someone, taking heaps of directions, so they are quite strong-willed when it comes to training. They are built to rely on their own nose and eyes, not for you to be their ears and nose. Which means that one of their biggest challenges can be controlling these senses. Many of these breeds are resigned to living their lives on long lines as their drive to hunt and chase is so strong, which seems rather sad when we have bred them for the exact opposite of that type of life. Examples of these kinds of dogs are the Beagle, the Bloodhound, the Dachshund and the Greyhound.

Working Group

These are breeds of dogs that have been created and selectively bred to perform and carry out tasks alongside us humans. This may be for herding sheep, sniffer-dog work, or search and rescue. These breeds have been designed to work. They are most certainly not suited to a quick loop of the park each day and then being left at home alone. Left without stimulation they can be distressed and destructive. They are at their best when able to put their power and focus into doing a job. Examples of these kinds of dogs are the Bernese Mountain Dog, the Boxer and the Doberman.

Gun dog (UK)/Sporting (US) Group

A highly intelligent, active and alert breed group that were created for their ability to be on duty, on the prowl, on the search for long shifts and stints of time. This group is made up of four types of dogs – the spaniels, the setters, the retrievers and the pointers. These are all breeds that work alongside people, taking direction but very, very intent on fulfilling a purpose – that is what they live for. A working Cocker is not just another name or type of breed of Cocker; it is a very specifically bred dog that is not suitable for most homes across the world. It is a dog that doesn't have an 'off' switch, that will go and go and go even when you think it's not possible. So imagine a dog like this in your home, when you are trying to get the kids bathed and get dinner on the table. Examples of these kinds of dogs are the Hungarian Vizsla, the German Short-haired Pointer and the Weimaraner.

Terrier Group

Generally bred to seek out and kill or catch animals such as badgers, rabbits and rats. These are tenacious dogs bred to be determined, forthright and not afraid of going into any situation. This group has a wide span of breeds, from the Staffordshire Bull Terrier to the Irish Terrier, so there is a huge array and variety within this breed group, but you should still not lose sight of their instincts to run into things – their 'why-go-around-something-when-you-can-go-through-it?' personalities. I find these breeds can be mouthy in playing and quick to snap if their thresholds aren't managed and they aren't channelled appropriately. Examples of this breed group are the Irish Terrier, the Pit Bull Terrier and the Border Terrier.

Herding (UK)/Pastoral (US) Group

Originally created to help humans herd, move and often protect livestock. So their co-ordination is usually quick, their ability to think for themselves is high, they can be out and about for very long periods of time, and some can be described as frantic in nature as they need to be able to look, listen, see and respond all in very quick succession. So these traits may not always make them the most relaxing to live with, as their drives can be very high. Examples of this breed group are the Belgian Malinois, Border Collie and the Old English Sheepdog.

Utility Group

I always find this a strange grouping as the mix is so huge! Generally speaking, though, this grouping is dogs that are supposed to be 'useful' to us but not from working lineage. They are supposed to be beneficial to humans, such as the Dalmatian who used to serve firefighters (personally I'd classify this as Working) or the French Bulldog (which I would put in the Terrier group by nature). So don't be disillusioned that the breeds in this grouping are easier; you still need to look at them individually. A Dalmatian is very different from a Frenchie! Examples of dogs within this breed group are the English Bulldog, the Akita and the Chow Chow.

Toy Group

This group was created for the smaller breed of dogs. However, don't be under any illusions that smaller or the word 'toy' means they may not have challenges or may be cuddlier or more biddable in nature. In this group you have the Miniature Pinscher and the Toy Poodle. These are utterly incomparable in nature or creation. This group, I feel, is a rather lazy grouping as they are so much more than just their size. Examples of breeds in this group are the Pomeranian, the Toy Poodle (yet the Standard Poodle would go into the working-dog section) and the Cavalier King Charles Spaniel.

Crossbreeds

When we come to make our breed selections or crossbreed selections, we need to be really brutal with our decision-making process, as this is actually the stage where it can be doomed or where you fly – because you are keeping your abilities, desires and realities in mind.

If you are considering a crossbreed, this doesn't automatically mean you get the best bits of both of those breeds. You might do, but if you choose incorrectly from the litter or an awful breeder, you may get the absolute worst parts. For the last few years, we as behaviourists have started to see this with the crossbreed of the Cockapoo.

The Cockapoo has soared in popularity, due to its teddy-bear looks and people's belief that it is hypoallergenic and easy. When in fact the opposite is now the case.

The Cocker Spaniel is designed to work in the field, working for long hours, to be up and down, in and out. The Poodle is designed to do water retrieval work, is very adaptable and loves people. None of those descriptions scream 'easy' or 'suitable for everyone', yet thousands if not millions of this breed are circulating in the world right now. The main reason being because of their size, their look and the fact that their coat does not shed (it does matt, though). Which should highlight to you how we as humans are actually making our decisions on which dog should join our family. Not through their actual suitability of personality, activity levels or personality type, but on the coat type and the fluffy look.

A personal list of six brilliant breeds to consider for a family dog:

1. Norfolk Terrier – a joyful, fun-loving and friendly little dog who has made the transition into family homes really well. They have heaps of personality, love to be out and about, and are adaptable companions for everyone.
2. Miniature Poodle – there is a reason the Poodle is being crossed with everything under the sun, because it is an exceptional little pal – friendly, playful and affectionate. I also find them to be really quick learners. They can be barky, though, and you need to be aware of this when looking for one to share your life with.
3. Smooth-coated Collie – loyal, affectionate and loving

35

but also very clever and love to be in among it all in family life. They are on the vulnerable breed list (i.e. at risk of disappearing) as they are not as popular as they used to be, which seems a real shame. They do like to alert-bark at the door. They are very different from the Border Collie, which is a much more high-maintenance working dog. They can be super-sensitive but are very quick to learn.

4. Retired Greyhound – I don't understand why more people don't take on these gorgeous dogs. They love to chill, enjoy minimal exercise and sleep all day. They have been bred to chase and kill small furry animals, so are not suited to living with cats or other small pets.

5. Leonberger – a giant dog known for being calm, steady and friendly. Some can be wary of strangers, but if you find the right breeder who is breeding for character and temperament, you will have hit the jackpot. Due to it being a giant breed, you will need to work extremely hard on the control elements of owning a large dog.

6. Labrador – I just love them. A well-bred Labrador, not from working heritage, can be wonderful. They do moult though. Also bear in mind, the Chocolates tend to be 'sillier' in nature and behaviour, and less steady.

*Five breeds you should think carefully
about before bringing home*

I love all dogs, but believe that the right dog in the right home is the best solution for everyone. So the following list is not one of 'bad' breeds – there are no bad breeds – but the most common breeds that I see people selecting for all the wrong reasons. Please read this list carefully and ask yourself some honest questions about suitability before bringing a dog home based on just its looks.

- Hungarian Vizsla – people love the look of them, the smoothness, the ginger fur, the sleek appearance. Yet they pretty quickly realise they have taken on a dog who is designed to work, designed to be incredibly sensitive and vocal. A Vizsla doesn't just want to exercise but needs hours of it. Its brain is so clever that entertaining them can feel like a full-time job. To have a happy Vizsla, you need space, you need to accept the jumpy lamb-like quality of the way they behave, that they will talk to you and are certainly not silent or built for busy people or busy households, because they need such a huge dedication of time.
- Smooth-haired Miniature Dachshund – people select them due to their size, due to their cuteness, and that their ability to be picked up and carried in cities makes them a so-called easy choice. Yet owners don't understand the barking nature of this breed. There is no quiet version of this dog. Do not then ask me how to stop your dog from barking at people, dogs, cats,

literally anything that walks the planet! These dogs were designed to disappear underground. That bark was needed to alert people to what they had found. That bark originally had a purpose.

- Cockapoo – hugely popular now across the globe but many are frantic, vocal dogs who cannot cope with being left alone. The Cocker Spaniel is a clever dog and so is the Poodle. They need stimulation, not hours alone on the sofa. I see far too many Cockapoos with obsessive hypervigilant behaviours, barking their heads off as they can't cope with the world they are living in. Any Cockapoo bred from a working Cocker will likely exhibit stressful, high drive behaviours that make living with them hard.

- Rottweiler and German Shepherd – many select these because they are big dogs, perhaps they grew up with them when they were younger. Or they are just drawn to the powerhouses they are. However, they are both guarding, working breeds, so the level of commitment and work they need from you in order to cope with modern busy lives is huge. The biting, nipping puppy phases can feel so much more intense with big, powerful dogs with big heads and mouths, but often people do not consider this. A jumping Rottie puppy who grabs your coat as they bite and teethe will feel intimidating in comparison to a Pomeranian giving it a go.

- Golden Retriever – I've seen it time and time again, where people assume the Retriever to be the kind of 'easy' option, that everyone loves a Retriever. Yet the maturity period I see in them is long – two to three years. Of course they can be loving and affectionate, but for those three years of growing up they can also be silly, wild and it can feel like you are banging your head against a brick wall. One of my client's Retrievers, in his first two years, dislocated her shoulder, pulled her over and she ended up having to have surgery on her back due to the exuberance he had demonstrated!

So that was quite a lot to take in! But choosing the right dog is the most important part of dog ownership, and worth your care, attention and understanding. I urge you to invest proper time and energy in the search for a canine companion to share your life. When you choose wisely, and feel really happy with the dog you have decided to bring home, all of the next steps become so much easier. Set yourself, and your dog, up for success from day one.

PART TWO

Bringing the Right Dog Home

CHAPTER THREE

The Reality Check

I think it is worth pointing out that, while life with a dog can be the most rewarding, enjoyable and fun experience, it can also be overwhelming, tiring and frustrating. Many's the puppy owner who has asked themselves, guiltily, if they've made a terrible mistake. I myself have been through all of these emotions. From fostering dogs, to owning a puppy, taking in rescue dogs to share my life and working with thousands of dogs across the years, I think I have pretty much seen it all.

I have turned up at people's homes and they have answered the door in tears of overwhelm and frustration. I've had to work with a client to help them make the decision to have a five-month-old puppy put to sleep due to him having bitten multiple people, some of them to the point of needing stitches – this was not simple teething. I have worked with certified dangerous dogs and had to cuddle my clients when their frustrations ran so deep at the decisions they had made and were now stuck with, when their life could have been made easier if more work had been put into choosing the right dog.

I believe it is important to be honest and realistic with people about the demands of dog and puppy ownership. It's not all sunshine, rainbows and pretty pictures on Instagram, and we do a disservice to our dogs by suggesting it's easy, especially at the beginning. So the stories I share here are not designed to put you off dog ownership, but to help make the right, informed decisions for you and your family or set-up.

Owning a puppy or taking on a rescue dog can be marvellous. I remember going to collect our bulldog Cookie as a puppy; it was one of the best days of my life. My husband and I had dreamed about this moment for years. The joy, friendship, love and play you receive from living with a dog is incredible. Dogs can raise you up, make you appreciate the seasons, see the world through different eyes and make you realise what an incredible species they really are. Your dog will stand by your side every waking day, greeting you like no other person in your life does. They will be with you through thick and thin. Our bulldog saw us through our lives as newlyweds, my nanny dying, the miraculous birth of my nephew, the birth of my own two children, the setting up of my business and much more besides. She knew me better than some of my own family members. This partnership is truly the best thing ever, but it isn't always easy.

The tiring, sleepless nights of puppy ownership, the navigation of responsibility if you are unused to it, can come as a shock. When the teething begins, and you realise that your fluffy puppy has turned into a baby shark whose sole intention is to get their needle teeth into every item and surface you possess, including your own body.

When you discover that just because you love your rug, velvet sofa and armchairs, it doesn't mean your puppy or rescue dog has any respect for them. I constantly meet new owners who are having to drastically revise their expectations of what having a dog looks like. This all takes time.

Taking on an older dog doesn't mean you sidestep problems either. Many people underestimate the time and effort that is necessary, especially if taking in a rescue dog, to understand the impact its experiences, previous owners and environments will have had on the dog that they bring home.

There is a great movement called 'adopt, don't shop' that you frequently see on social media posts. The sentiment is a great one, but my main focus to improve dogs' lives would be on the fact that we should be reducing the amount of poorly bred dogs in the world, reducing the need for dogs to be given up or put to sleep. However, as a dog behaviourist, my main concern is to make sure people end up with the right dog for their life, whether that is a rescue dog, a puppy or a puppy rescue dog. The reality is that if we take on the right dog in the beginning, that dog should never end up in a rescue centre or, worse, put down simply for being unsuitable.

Good people can make bad choices when it comes to dog ownership. They wholeheartedly believe, often encouraged by social media, that love will cure everything. I genuinely wish this were true. But the truth is that a badly bred, badly socialised dog or puppy will impact your life in ways you never dreamed possible. The wrong dog in the wrong situation can create distress, anguish and tears – whether that be down to the veterinary costs, the behavioural problems that make this dog impossible to live with, or the fact that the dog hates every member of your family, won't step outside the house and is terrified of strangers. A client contacted me saying they had taken on a dog via a rescue centre in Turkey. She had lived with the dog for over six months and still couldn't get it to leave the house. Understanding what you are potentially taking on is crucial, and knowing that an issue may never be resolved is an important aspect to also come to terms with.

The lack of research that I'm seeing has a gigantic impact on the dogs I'm being contacted about. People sometimes think that a puppy is a blank slate, arriving with you fresh and free of problems. But a dog bred from an ill mother, raised in a hovel of a concrete cell, with no human or social interaction, is not going to thrive in the big wide world of real life. By the time you have realised this, that puppy breeder won't be answering your calls any more, they won't be there to help you and they definitely won't care. Your cash will have cleared through their bank account and they will be well on their way to welcoming another appallingly bred litter into the world to flog on, and so it continues. But it doesn't have to continue. We, as the consumer, as owners, have the power. We are the people searching for a best friend. So let's put the legwork into it that it deserves.

In the following pages I'm going to give you all the tools you need to identify the kind of dog that will work for the life you live. I'll show you the questions to ask and the red flags to watch out for. I so understand the impulse to 'save' every sad-faced puppy or dog that you see online, but it is essential that you make the right choices, both for the dog and for yourself.

IS NOW THE RIGHT TIME?

A little bit like having children, there is never an ideal time to get a dog. However, I do believe that there are definitely times when you should actively avoid taking on a dog! And here are a few of them:

- You work full-time and will be out of the house for long hours. This often raises eyebrows when I say it, as in this day and age we have daycare facilities, we have dog walkers, we have people we can pay to take our dog and look after them for extended periods every day. But for me, this isn't a reason to actually go out and get a dog. That is more like having a fluffy toy in the corner that you can just pet when you walk in and then sit down with a glass of wine. It won't fulfil the dog or you. Dogs are not designed to live lonely, solitary lives; they need interaction. And they also don't enjoy being passed from pillar to post. So while you may have desires to own a dog, it truly is your responsibility to look at the situation from a dog's perspective, not just your own.

    Daycare providers will tell you it's fine, that lots of their clients do this. As my mum used to say to me, 'If your friend puts their head in the oven, would you?' And of course my answer was no. Just because others are doing it does not mean it's right for you and your dog. Long-term daycare, every single day, works for very few dogs for their entire lives. You would need to find a dog who is independent, doesn't thrive on

47

human company, doesn't want to spend lots of time with their people – which to me, doesn't sound like an ideal companion dog!

- You are struggling with one existing dog but believe that bringing a new dog in will resolve it. Usually it won't. You need to help your existing dog out before you think about bringing another dog into the fold.
- Your relationship feels at crisis point. A dog will not make it better. It will simply add in another stress point.
- You are just about to have a baby or adopt a child. At this point in your life, you should be aware that taking on a dog would generally not be advisable. Purely due to the logistical side of trying to settle into life as a parent, adding a dog into it will only complicate matters. Giving yourself time would be advisable.
- Your landlord will not permit it. You must seek permission before bringing a dog home. Please don't try to do it retrospectively.

You will note that I don't include things like the size of your flat, house or apartment, or whether or not you have a garden. The main reason being that, quite honestly, I don't think these are hugely important. Sadly, I feel that too many rescue centres place too much emphasis on the size of a home and the existence of a garden. Whereas my experience of living and working in a city like London and with clients in the States is that when we have less space, we often make more effort to get out and go places. So don't let the size of your space dictate your potential to live with a dog. It is about choosing the right type of dog to share your home.

My only caveat to that is to know that a garden does make life easier. For some breeds, like the busy working ones, a garden is a must.

When we took on a rescue Great Dane, he was 65 kilos and we lived as a family of four in a small London home, with a small garden. That didn't matter, though, as we did so much with him outside the house. The only thing I did have to do was teach my children, who were three and five years old at the time, that if Fred started running, they should throw themselves against the wall, as 65 kilos coming at you is a lot!

Of course space is a consideration. For instance, if you live in a tiny apartment with no outdoor space, taking on a Husky would be one of the worst ideas I've ever heard due to the fact that they enjoy being outside, prefer no central heating and need to be exercised for miles every day. But if you were considering a nine-year-old retired Greyhound, a breed that loves to sleep for hours every day, then I would definitely consider it.

In my opinion it isn't about what you own, where you live or how many bedrooms you have (do bear in mind, though, that more room can feel better when you have a puppy that wants to chew you all the time, or a dog who dislikes busy households). A bigger house doesn't make you a better prospect for a dog. It is the ability to create a home, a safe place for your dog, that is important. And then making the right choices about which kind of dog to bring into that home. This is how you set yourself up to succeed.

PUPPY OR RESCUE DOG?

If you are weighing up whether to get a puppy or a rescue dog, do not be under any illusion that one is better than the other. Do not be influenced by people telling you what they think you should be doing. Take advice from a behaviourist like myself, ask for their experience, and take on independent advice and help from someone who has no vested interest in the dog you take on. In my opinion there are a few key points to consider when making this key decision, and there are also some myths that need busting.

Puppies

Many clients come to me with the opinion that taking on a puppy is the easier and safer option than finding a rescue dog. This isn't factually true. A puppy can be an angel: lovable, snuggly, joyful and an amazing way to make you reassess all the things you spend your life doing. They are also tiring, pooing, weeing machines who will put holes in your jumpers, bite your toes and jump up at your kids with their mouths wide open.

All of this happens, of course, because they are exploring the world, they are learning, they are seeking out sensory input and figuring out what works and doesn't.

The early days of having a puppy can feel like you are on a roller coaster of ups and downs, highs and lows. There are days where things go well and then, the very next day, it feels like you have regressed a million steps. This is all completely 'normal', and you are not alone in those feelings. I have people describe their feelings as the 'puppy blues' where they realise the joyful event of getting a dog also comes with huge adjustment and that creates a sadness that they never expected.

If you feel that your mental health is truly being affected by the sudden change, do reach out to someone like me who can help you with your dog, and if you need to, find a therapist or consult your GP. Don't leave it; it may be that the puppy or the dog has triggered emotions, feelings, trauma or suppression of expression that you didn't even know you had or were going to go through. There is no right or wrong way to feel as we each come from different pasts, different situations and different households, and that has to be considered when we look at dealing with any life-changing event.

When choosing a puppy, you have to select the right breed or combination of breeds for you, find the right breeder, select the right puppy and then put in around two years of hard work to fully socialise it and integrate it into your life. On the other hand, a rescue dog often arrives fully grown and you will be given information on any areas that you may need to work on. So it really isn't as straightforward as a puppy being the better or easier option. But it does need to feel like the right decision for you, as it is you who needs to live with this being for the next twelve years. (God, I wish they lived longer!)

Rescue dogs

'But don't all rescue dogs have issues?' I'm always still surprised when this is people's perception and a genuine reason why they think they may not consider a rescue dog. We seem to have fallen into the trap of thinking that getting a puppy is the easy option, which is absurd, considering you are taking on a baby animal and raising it.

Rescue dogs, just like puppies, come in all shapes, sizes, varieties, personalities and with issues or non-issues. The key, just like taking on a puppy, is to select the right one for you. When it comes to choosing a rescue dog, you must not lose sight of this goal in the face of wanting to bring all the sad dogs home.

Rescue dogs come, like all of us, with previous experience of life – sometimes not all of it good. When you take on an older dog, you are usually told up front of the dog's issues and experiences. A rescue dog will have been assessed, and will come with information about their likes, dislikes and anxieties. So if you are presented with two dogs, one who has aggression issues towards humans due to a previous experience and one who doesn't, you can decide what is right for you, and where you want to concentrate your time and efforts.

A rescue dog may also come with medical needs or training needs. Any reputable rescue centre will let you know about these in advance, so you can make an informed decision. Trusting the rehoming centre is key, as their processes and their staff are the ones who will be assessing the dog and putting it into your home.

CHAPTER FOUR

How to Find the Right Breeder

A breeder is a breeder is a breeder, aren't they? They are much of a muchness, surely?

Never has there been a time where this has been less true. As we see the rise in dog ownership going through the roof thanks to the pandemic, thousands of people have been breeding dogs that are simply not suitable to be in family homes. One puppy farm I know of made around £2.4m per year out of selling dogs. They most certainly were not in it for the love.

The harsh and honest reality is that very few people who are breeding should actually be doing so. The breeding of a great, affectionate, confident and friendly dog should be at the forefront of a breeder's mind. Instead, we are seeing the exact opposite taking place, where people see breeding as a money-making venture, an easy way to hoodwink the public into paying thousands of pounds for a creature with very few questions asked.

As the value of owning a dog has gone up, so have the trickery and tactics being used by backyard breeders, puppy dealers, puppy farmers and licensed breeders.

It has become rather like watching a magic show: you know what they are doing isn't factually possible but you aren't allowed to ask questions. A client of mine actually got escorted by two big burly security people out of an apparent breeder's home for asking too many questions. I mean, the fact that someone had security at their supposed home is utterly baffling to me.

A decent breeder should be encouraging you, answering you, constantly updating you and thrilled with the level of interest you are showing. If they aren't engaged with the questions you are asking, and glad to have you asking them, then there is an issue. And even if that breeder isn't a dodgy one, why would you want to take a dog from someone who can't be bothered to answer your questions?

I'm pretty sure I've heard every trick in the book, but then deceptively clever criminals looking to make a quick buck come up with another way of doing things. Do not be deceived by those with show rosettes and credentials either. It isn't a guarantee that all is right in the world. There are so many factors to consider when searching for your breeder.

To give you an idea of some of the things people have been told and the depths to which people will plummet to snare people into buying a puppy from them:

- **'I can't send you any photos of the puppies until they are six weeks old as I don't touch them until they are that old.'**
  Never have I heard such nonsense. A home breeder would have those dogs in their house – many I know sit in the pen with the bitch and her brood, and

even have their morning cup of tea in with the puppies. Absolutely baffling to think this could ever be used as a reason. More likely that the puppies are sitting in a black hole of a farm, nowhere near where this person lives and they will only arrive in her home at seven to eight weeks old when she starts doing viewings because she is a dealer – a home that gets paid to house the puppies for selling purposes.

- **'That trembling is normal, all puppies do it.'**
  No they don't. A puppy who is that scared of the breeder or a person visiting is not one that you should be buying. Full stop.

- **'The dog is my mum's but I'm just here helping her.'**
  Usually a problem. The real owner would need to be at death's door to not meet the people potentially taking home one of the litter she would have spent hours, days, weeks rearing.

- **'All of that litter are sold but I've got some available from another litter.'**
  This is not a breeder being helpful. It is someone breeding literally shedloads of dogs to make sure they can earn as much money as possible.

- **'You can't touch the mother, she doesn't really like people.'**
  This is not a litter you want to be buying from. Your dog will end up exactly the same way. Walk away now.

- **'I don't know the father, I bought sperm online.'**
  This actually happened to a client of mine. Someone who gives that little thought to the breeding of their dog is not a breeder you want to be associated with or buying from. If their bitch was that precious, if they

adored her that much, so much forethought would be put into the creation of a litter within her.

- **'No, that is definitely the mother.'**
Yet in the photos there is a completely different-looking dog said to be the mother. This has happened to me and to clients on arrival at someone's home – where they have simply put a bitch in with a litter and it isn't the mother, because they are wise to the fact that people are being told to see a litter with the mother. It isn't as simple as that any more either.

- **'You can't use the loo, I'm afraid. I don't like people walking around my house.'**
This is a very strange thing to say to someone who has travelled miles to assess a litter for suitability. There will be a reason, probably because either the home isn't theirs and they are simply using it as a façade to place a litter in for viewings. Or they are hiding other litters, other dogs or something more sinister. If it were a real family home, there would be nothing to hide. I've also turned up at a house before with a client and the 'breeders' have wanted us to view the litter outside the house, on the lawn, and not enter the home. We set off straight back home.

- **'You need to pay a deposit but the account isn't in my name.'**
Usually because it isn't their litter. Or you will be asked to pay cash with no refunds permitted. You can consider reporting a breeder like this to HMRC.

- **'It's Darcy's second litter'** – **when the dog isn't called Darcy.**
The changing of names, forgetting of names, a dog

appearing to not answer to a name, are all signs that the supposed owner or breeder has no idea what they are talking about. And the dog very likely does not belong to them.

- **'The dog is pedigree and had all of its tests done, but I can't show you the paperwork as it isn't here with me right now.'**

  Don't accept that it will be posted to you, or texted to you. You want to be able to trace a family line that the paperwork is real, not copied or made up, which is increasingly happening. Paperwork is being fraudulently given, created by clever breeders, and new owners don't question it. Not that a pedigree is the be all and end all, but if you are saying you are breeding from a pedigree bitch and sire, you should have the relevant paperwork and testing documents to accompany the dogs you have used for the litter.

- **'The photos of the pups in the advert were taken in another house; that's why it looks different from where we are now.'**

  No decent breeder would be shipping their dog and puppies to other premises for the sake of photographs.

All in all, you can see there are so many reasons people give, so many lies that are told and so many deceitful practices taking place on a daily basis across the country. It really is up to you to be honest with yourself, and to decide on whether waiting for the 'right' dog is worth it or whether it's best to just rush in and hope for the best.

I see the end product of those who hope for the best or those who choose to turn a blind eye, to pretend that what the breeder has done is acceptable. People will tell themselves all kinds of lies to move forward with a purchase. I just urge you to weigh up the long-term effect of taking on a badly bred dog. It may change your life for ever.

Some breeders will ask people to simply select a puppy on the basis of its colour and sex. Just because they ask you to do this doesn't mean it's right. When I talk to breeders on a client's behalf, and this is their selection route, I move on straight away, as I know the breeder isn't for me or my client. I am looking to have a discussion on the mother's personality, to discuss how the breeder describes each puppy within the litter to help make an informed choice. And yes, that can mean that a search takes a lot longer, but try not to lose sight of how big this decision is and the impact it can have on your life, in a good way or an awful way.

Once you are actually talking to someone about a litter, they should want to quiz you; it should feel like an interview. And in return you should be quizzing them back as you have a great deal to find out. Here are just some of the questions I have at the top of my list or in the back of my mind when I'm talking to breeders at the very start of the puppy process:

Can I hear the dogs in the background?
If you can hear barking and squabbling, then be prepared for your puppy to be a barker too. You may want to ask (politely) why the barking is happening as it could

be relevant when you think about the dog you may end up living with. There is a big difference between dogs who are barking because someone is at the door and dogs who are barking for attention or who are just very vocal, loud dogs.

Why did they breed from mum?

Is this their business? Is it because they adore her so much they want more pups? Is it for shows or to work them? It is important to understand the reasoning so you can decide whether it is the breeder for you. Personally, I'd be looking for someone who feels their dog has such a great nature and health that it should be passed on.

Who lives in that household?

Humans, other dogs, other animals? If your puppy is going to live with children, it is helpful if they come from a home where they have at least encountered children before. Ditto other pets, like cats.

Where are the puppies being raised?

Utility room, kitchen, stable, conservatory? If you are planning on having a dog live with you in your home, then being raised in the home from birth is very important. This way the puppies don't bat an eyelid when they hear the radio, the phone ring, the washing machine on a full cycle or a cupboard door slam. These are all part and parcel of everyday family life, but could be distressing for a puppy who has been raised in a stable, for instance.

Was dad a stud or a beloved dog of a friend?
Ask the breeder to describe the dad's personality. Try to understand why that mating was chosen. Or was it a happy accident? Is the male a desirable sire (father to the litter)? These are important things to know and be aware of, as you want to make sure that you feel your breeder has conducted their due diligence. A happy accident isn't necessarily a bad thing as it's how many of the crossbreeds years ago came about, but you do want to make sure that you like what you see or hear about when it comes to the father. Show breeders will tell you about the father's show credentials, but this will be irrelevant to most of us.

What does mum like doing if she didn't have the litter to take care of?
For example, do they say she's a busy dog, she loves to be out and about, she follows them everywhere, etc.? All of these may be small indicators, as 'following you everywhere' means 'needy', 'a busy dog' means 'on the go, never rests'. Refer back to your checklist of what your dog needs to be.

Are they open to you having an early selection of a puppy?
It's so important not to just take the one that is left. You want to ensure that you get the one that is best suited to you, not just the one that is available. This is a choice that will affect the next decade of your life, if not more.

When a breeder says there is no difference in puppies, all of mine are very good and have great personalities, be cautious. There is still a sliding scale of suitability. Plus, I've met and worked with dogs who were described this way by a breeder, and it certainly isn't always true. You need to have a part in the decision process; once that dog is handed over, it is yours and not the breeder's. A decent, experienced breeder should know their puppies inside and out, and understand the tiny differences within that litter. Even if it is a balanced litter, I still want a choice.

Things you would want to see at a breeder's home:

- That the mother of the litter is welcoming, happy, healthy and has no behavioural issues – e.g. barking, aggression, doesn't like being touched, kept out of the room from you, etc. I've had cases where a breeder won't let go of a dog's collar or allow it to come over to say hi. This isn't a good sign. Do make sure that you genuinely also believe the dog to be the actual mother of the litter, not just placed there to show you.
- That it is a family home, where you can see evidence of a dog's presence and a dog who is part of the family. Unless you are seeking a working dog who will be purely for working purposes and will also live outside in a warm kennel, the puppies should be indoors and part of the family home.
- You should have the feeling that you would want to take the mother of the litter home with you. If you wouldn't, then you certainly shouldn't be taking one of her puppies! You should love the nature of the pup's mother, as it will strongly influence the temperament of her puppies.

- A pen where the puppies are kept, with access to different surfaces and toys. You need to see that they are well catered for. You should expect a bit of mess in terms of toileting accidents, but it shouldn't be utterly filthy or squalid and the breeder's home shouldn't stink. The pen should be within the home. If it's a sunny day, you may find that the breeder has pens set up in the home and in the garden and both should look utilised. Beware if the one in the home is perfect and immaculate, because it suggests the puppies are kept outside most of the time.

- The puppies should ideally be fed separately rather than from one bowl, as this can increase competition around resources. If they are being fed from one bowl, you want to see that there is food left over so that there is never the case where a dog has to miss out on food due to the competition between littermates. Competition over food may result in a dog who is overprotective of their food, which can be dangerous.

- If there are children in the house, ensure that the dogs are not overhandled by them as this can create issues later on where the dog wants to avoid kids due to the handling they experienced in the primary socialisation period. It can be why sometimes visiting grandchildren of a breeder can be ideal as it allows just the right amount of contact.

- The breeder should demonstrate a genuine sense of love and pride for the litter but not an overwhelming sense of attachment where they could have already created separation-anxiety-related issues for those puppies.

- You should feel comfortable within their home and garden, even if the style or décor may not be to your tastes. You should feel at ease.
- The breeder should be sending you consistent updates, with videos and images.
- The breeder of any pedigree dog – and this applies to those breeding crossbreeds too – should be able to show you any certificates for hip scores, medical tests and registrations. You should be shown so that you can do your research afterwards to check their validity. These certificates should be originals, and should not look scanned in or photocopied.
- If there are any pedigree names on the charts, the breeder should not object to you checking that these tables, charts and certificates actually apply to the dogs you are seeing in front of you.
- A good breeder should be able to give you feedback on each puppy, so you can describe the kind of dog you are dreaming of and they can help match you. They will be living with those puppies day in and day out. A dog who 'chooses you' isn't necessarily the right dog for your family, it is just the most willing to push forward and away from its littermates. That can be great for some people and not for others.

Things you do not want to see at a breeder's home:

- A dog or dogs who appear worried or scared of the breeder. You definitely do not want to see any fearful behaviour of any kind – a dog (whether the mum or the pups) who doesn't want to be held, a dog who doesn't want contact, or a dog who tries to get away or hides at the back or under things is never a good sign. Even if a puppy is handed to you and eventually nestles in for a cuddle, it still isn't one I'd be considering taking into my home.

- A mother or father (or both) who are aggressive, reactive, unwelcoming or difficult. That does not bode well for you and the potential puppy. Try not to convince yourself that the barking or the fear wasn't that bad. It will be far worse if you have to live with it for the next decade or more.

- Dogs who are barking, shouting and throwing themselves at the front door.

- A litter that is kept away from the home. They cannot learn what the home means if they aren't living within it.

- A dirty, badly kept litter in terms of hygiene and set-up – I'm less worried about the décor or cleanliness of their actual home. You do not need to like their decorative style, but you do need to think the way they raise their dogs is excellent.

- Lots of dogs of differing breeds with their own litters or who are pregnant. If it is a family breeder, there should be only one bitch with a litter. If it is a professional breeder such as someone involved in showing their dogs, you may have a couple of litters due around the same time. However, this should not be a regular occurrence and you wouldn't want the dogs to be mated over and over again. You also don't want to see bitches being mated too young, e.g. one year old and younger. Do ask about how many litters the

bitch has had. They may not be truthful, though!
- A licence to have multiple breeding bitches. Just because they are licensed does not make it OK. It just means the council is aware they have multiple dogs to breed from and make money from. You should be able to search to see how many dogs they are licensed for. Some I have looked at have been licensed for up to 350 dogs. This is literally a puppy farm; it is just licensed by the council.
- Someone who won't let you into the home or property (no matter what the excuse, they knew you were coming!). If they have something to hide from you, this isn't a person to entrust with raising a puppy that you will have in your home for years.

When it comes to actually selecting a puppy from a litter, if you cannot get the one you want, be prepared to walk away. It should be as simple as that. Do not settle or be persuaded to take a different one. It's a tough thing to walk away from a huddle of adorable puppies, but it will be worth it in the end when you find the right one.

During the selection process, you must refer back to the original document you created in terms of what you wanted in a dog. If the puppy is to be a companion to your children, then you should be selecting the one who naturally comes and seeks out your children. You definitely do not want to be choosing the one trying to get away. If you are seeking a quiet companion to be by your side while you sit and read, you really don't want the one who pushes all the litter out of the way to climb onto your lap and bite your chin.

Many breeders will say that you cannot tell a dog's personality when they are so young, but I disagree. You may not be able to tell their exact nature, but you can start to see snippets and indicators and good puppy selection is about using these to make the best decision you can. So that when you bring your new puppy home, you have already chosen them in such a way that they are set up to succeed. And now you begin your side of the work, raising them in the way to best suit your family.

CHAPTER FIVE

Selecting and Finding a Rescue Dog

I've found through my work with clients across the UK, the US and Australia that finding a rescue dog can sometimes feel more daunting than a puppy search. However, it is worth noting there are now some brilliant breed-specific rescues that exist, who have such a wealth of knowledge and can really help you. To give you an idea what a brilliant job these breed-specific rescues are doing in the UK, the Kennel Club estimate that these specific rescues are responsible for rehoming over 10,000 dogs per year. And that is just the figures from the ones that are affiliated with the KC.

In addition to this, there are rehoming charities who will also have assessed the dogs they have in their care. There is also the option of private rehoming, as well as websites that allow owners to advertise their own dogs as being up for rehoming. Be careful with these types of sites as the information given about each dog is just based on the opinion of someone who's giving the dog away. The dog has not been independently assessed. The current owner may tell you anything to get rid of the dog.

You must exercise caution when you begin the search for a rescue dog. You should be placing as much importance, time and effort into sourcing and finding the most suitable dog for you and your set-up as you would if you were getting a puppy. To give you an example, it took me nearly five months to help a very well-known name find his first rescue dog. We saw many lovely dogs in that time, but none that were right for him and the life he leads.

One benefit of looking for a rescue dog rather than a puppy is that you can see in front of you what you are getting. Once you've met a rescue dog, I find you can make a decision pretty easily. I'm not talking about just going on an internet advert or description. For example, if the rehoming website lists a dog who needs a great deal of exercise per day, who cannot be left alone and is destructive when separated, you know right away whether that is something you feel ready to take on. Whereas if a breeder advertises their puppies in that way, would you still go ahead?! Disreputable breeders will tell you whatever you want to hear, while good rescue homes have a very different attitude. It is not in their interest to lie to you because they are not making thousands of pounds from you taking the dog on. If they mislead you about a dog's nature, they run the risk of you returning the dog, or holding them responsible for any damage the dog causes. A bad breeder or puppy farmer or dealer will simply disappear and you won't be able to trace them.

It may be helpful here to insert some commonly used terms on rehoming websites and kennel doors, so you can read between the lines of what the kennel staff are telling you.

'Excitable' – Bouncy, energetic, on the go all the time.

'Needs a quiet home' – That means few visitors: this is a dog that does not love lots of people.

'Big character' – Be prepared for mischief and mayhem.

'Cheeky' – Won't be told what to do!

'Talkative' or 'chatty' – Barks a lot or is very vocal.

'Ongoing management' – There is a behavioural issue that may never be fully resolved. This usually needs an experienced owner and is not a great first dog for someone.

'Protective' – May guard, bark and lunge.

'Loves to join in' – Could be needy and not leave you alone.

This is not to say that you should dismiss dogs with any of the characteristics above, but it's important to go into meeting rescue dogs with your eyes and ears fully open.

So first things first, you refer to your list from page 18 and you do not deviate from it! If, for example, you have your heart set on an affectionate, quiet, family-friendly dog, you do not then opt for the independent, doesn't-like-human-contact breed or dog that you find in the rescue home, no matter how much you fall in love with it, or feel sorry for it. I cannot stress how crucial it is to stick to your original list.

You will not get everything you want; no dog is perfect, in the same way no human is either. However, we do need to prioritise the characteristics that sit at the top of our lists.

To give you some idea of the process, when I was searching for our most recent rescue dog, I did an inventory of where our family life was at that exact moment. If I describe my life, it might make a bit more sense to you and you can then picture your own life and what you may like or want.

My job as a dog behaviourist meant that I was perfectly happy to take a dog that needed a bit of training. That didn't faze me at all. However, we had recently lost our rescue Great Dane and I knew that I didn't have the time to put into a tricky dog right now; he'd had his own issues as he'd had four homes before we took him on. My children were five and seven years old and were desperate for us to get a Labrador puppy. However, my five-year-old has sensory processing disorder and we were just getting to grips with the initial impact of this. I knew that neither she nor I would be able to cope with the demands of a puppy at this time in our lives. She would want to constantly manhandle it due to the SPD and I just couldn't give a puppy what it required and be able to help her as well. My husband and I are both self-employed, and a dog would need to fit in around that. We live in East London, in a busy part of town but with a lot of access to green space. We have a small garden, cats and a tortoise, so an acceptance of other animals was crucial. Having lived with our darling deaf bulldog, the idea of taking on another deaf dog, or a blind one, didn't worry me. Living with a 65-kilo Great Dane also didn't faze us – so size, fur type and what it looked like really did not matter. The key to everything for us was the personality.

Our list looked like this:

Enjoys being around children

Has lived with or could live with cats

Comfortable being left alone for short periods

Not reactive to other dogs or people

Affectionate

Has the ability to be out and about for decent periods of time

Not a puppy (we knew our rescue needed to be two years old or over).

The things I really wasn't bothered about and that didn't matter to me:

Coat type – long, short, shedding or not

Size of dog

What it looked like

Whether it was recall trained

Whether it was loose-lead trained

Didn't need to be able to live with other dogs

If it alert-barked e.g. at the door

Whether it was deaf or blind.

Once you've identified what you want from a rescue dog, the initial steps of how to actually begin your search often feel like the hardest. This is how I would begin . . .

Visit a verified rehoming centre and go to every single kennel and read every single description. Do not miss any dog out. I would like you to be reading the information, rather than judging the dog inside that kennel by what it looks like. If you are looking online at this rehoming centre's website, then you do the same, you click on every single dog's picture and you read every single dog's description. And you make a shortlist of the ones who match your criteria. And then you request to go and meet them.

It may take months of visiting and searching before any matches come up. Do not despair and just clutch at straws. Do not be tempted to give up and just cut corners.

I took my rescue Great Dane, Fred, on from Great Dane Care, who were an incredible breed-specific rescue centre. They knew exactly what we were looking for and we kept talking regularly, so that I was always at the forefront of their mind when dogs came in.

You *must* go and meet your future dog. I cannot express how important this is. I wish I could tell you how many dogs I have met who have arrived from abroad and are the polar opposite of the website description that sold them. I see it time and time again, where people lose faith or a search for a puppy or a rescue dog is taking too long, so they want to shortcut it. As we know from the story of the Hare and the Tortoise, the shortcut never wins. If you are looking at rehoming a dog from abroad, you need heaps and heaps of feedback. I'd be submitting lists of questions and asking for videos and photos. I often assess videos for clients, to give my feedback on what I see. It is really worth the time.

You must meet your potential dog and see if there is a natural connection, even if there is still work to be done to build on it. When searching for a rescue dog with a client of mine, I found the perfect one on paper; it literally ticked every single box. We arrived at the centre to meet the dog. I walked out with this beautiful boy, but there was just no interest, no connection and you can't overestimate the need for that to make it work and to draw you in hook, line and sinker! That dog needs to become your obsession, the one you would feel absolutely crestfallen about if some-one else got to him first.And sometimes that will happen. I had that last year. I fell in love with a gorgeous rescue dog, but we got pipped to the post by a woman who ran a cattle ranch with acres of land and was at home all day. I mean, I would happily go and live with that woman myself, so I can't blame the rescue for choosing her over me!

One of the biggest things to remember when you go and visit a dog in a rescue centre is that the kennel environment is hugely, gigantically stressful for a dog. It will not bring out the best in them and it will not make them perform and lure them into showing you their most impressive personalities. Did you know that black dogs are the hardest to rehome, as we, as humans, find it hard to read their emotions? Most of these dogs in rescue centres are stressed out, upset and feeling very sad indeed. If they were once a loved pet, their lives have changed and they have no understanding of why. So when you pass the kennel with the dog curled up in its bed, asleep and not engaging with you, do not just discount it. The dog may be in shutdown mode, and it may be too weary to show an interest in its new life, which is why it's sleeping all day. If you can, try to talk to the actual kennel staff, the people who are seeing these dogs day in and day out. They are the ones who see the best and worst sides of each dog, so ask them for feedback. Or stand back and just watch the dog you are interested in. Observe their interactions with kennel staff, watch them get walked and played with. This will give you more insight than speaking to the reception staff, who won't have that close daily contact.

Lastly, do not be pushed or coerced into taking on a dog due to its sob story. I know that this sounds awful to say, but as well as the dog being the right fit for you, you must be the right fit for the dog. It can feel terrible saying 'no' to a dog you have been offered. However, you must make it clear why you think that dog isn't right for your family. During our search, we were offered a wonderful little Springer Spaniel in rescue. She could live with kids, dogs, in fact any animal, so she was perfect on that front. However, her energy levels and her frantic way of approaching life (very common for spaniels) were the exact opposite of what we needed – so I had to say thank you but no thank you. A puppy must fit your life as well as the other way around, and it would have been unkind of us to take on a dog whose boundless energy was too much for our situation.

SETTLING IN A RESCUE DOG

I will never forget picking up Fred, our rescue Great Dane for the first time. He allowed himself to be loaded into our old Land Rover, his coat full of dandruff, doing what I asked but with no idea who I was. I had to kind of pick him up and help him in. The memory of his big trusting face peering back at me in the rear-view mirror as we drove the hours it took to get back to London still makes me want to cry. On the other hand, Pip, our most recent rescue dog, panted and drooled with stress the entire way home. The car wasn't a particularly familiar place to him, and he was anxious about the whole experience. It's times like those when I wish we could talk to and explain things to our dogs.

Online videos often suggest that the moment a dog gets its 'forever home' everything is perfect. The truth is that, for many rescue dogs, the rehoming process can feel quite a shocking time. Very often there isn't the option for rehoming centres and charities to do a huge amount of work to prepare the dog for the transition from kennels to living in a family home. Once they have found the right owner match, they just need to get the dogs out in order to make room for more dogs needing their help. Many charities are now trying to do a 'home from home' type of service, where the dog transitions from kennels to a foster home and then on to its owner, as the transition becomes easier for everyone involved. In some cases, the home from home will be the actual original owner's, to reduce the stress even more. The Blue Cross actively do this and make it clear online which dogs are still in the original homes.

Change is exhausting and often the best way for a dog to process it is to shut down and go to bed, to process everything through being still and quiet. We do need to be led by each dog, but I would always recommend that you have a safe, quiet place for your dog to sleep as soon as it comes home, and keep children and other pets well away. For some dogs who have been living in kennels, this may be the first time that they actually get the peace, space and quiet they need to rest. For at least the first few days, if not the full first week, allow the rescue dog to rest and sleep, to stay in their bed if they choose to. Never try to force interaction that the dog is not yet ready for. Also bear in mind, frantic dogs may feel the same stress but become more full on and less able to rest.

I want to reassure you that this sleeping and withdrawing is not problematic behaviour from a new rescue dog. This is a processing period, a learning curve and they must be left alone to do it.

The night we brought Fred home, once the children were in bed, my husband and I just sat in the kitchen with him, at the table, letting him come to us if he wanted. We had created a huge, bedded area within a recess of our kitchen, tucked away so that Fred wasn't in any walkways but so he felt like he could hear and see what he needed to. I considered sleeping downstairs next to him, but he seemed to want to be alone (by which I mean he wasn't being forthcoming, he wasn't looking for petting or interaction with us), so we decided to let him be on his own. We set up a baby monitor so that he could still hear us all and so we could monitor him. He lay curled on his big bed, not in a relaxed sleeping position, merely trying to hide away from it all. Resting but not in a confident, comfortable way.

If you have children, ideally the first week with a rescue dog would be one where the kids are at school or in nursery. The less commotion there is to begin with, the better. This isn't always possible, but if you can manage it, I would try. Set your expectations very low and you won't be disappointed.

Depending on the dog and its background, I often say to clients that I wouldn't attempt to walk the rescue dog for the first week at least. We don't need to throw everything at them at the same time and expect them to cope with it all. We should be aiming to keep the first week super simple, for the dog to learn where to toilet, to encourage them to eat and feel comfortable with a location to eat and drink from, to rest and observe from their bed and be left alone. Lastly, to start to see if they want to play or interact at all, allowing them to come to you. If you do feel like they have energy to burn, try playing in your garden, or a shared garden. I would only consider a walk if you really, honestly feel that they are open to it and are looking to expand their horizons. Even just try sitting together on your front doorstep as a starting point.

Do not try to tempt a new rescue dog out of a crate, pen or bed. They will emerge when they are ready. Just because you want to speed things up won't make it any more enjoyable for the dog. They have to figure a great deal out before they may even consider picking up a toy, taking a chew or interacting with you to ask for a stroke or a touch on the body.

Try to make the days predictable for the dog. Give them a reliable routine to grip on to while they are learning about you all and about their new home. Keep feed times regular, toileting trips, times when you sit on the floor near them should they decide to come over and seek you out. These are all little things but, if they happen every day, they can form a reassuring pattern for a dog, who then knows what to expect from its new environment.

Do not be overly worried if your dog will not eat at first. Anxiety and fear can halt even the most eager of appetites. Do make sure that what you are offering is something they are used to, even if it isn't what you want to feed them in the long term. Consistency is important at this time. I would keep them on the rehoming centre, or foster carer's, diet for the first seven to ten days, and then you can begin the process of moving them on to something better if you desire.

Do not be tempted to invite friends over, children or family, no matter how much they may want to come and meet your new pal. The last thing you want to do is overwhelm your dog, creating the possibility of them then reacting adversely to someone who needs to feature heavily in your life, purely because the dog felt overwhelmed and out of place.

With Pip, our rescue Smooth-coated Collie, I didn't take him to meet my extended family until we had had him in our home for two months. And even when I did for the first time, I simply met my mum out on a dog walk, just her and me. Then I came back home with him. After he had been in our lives for around three months, we visited my parents' home with my sister and her kids too. We also had baby gates put up so that separation could be easily done, should the need arise.

A RESCUE DOG TIMELINE

It's good to be prepared about how long it takes to settle in a rescue dog. If you keep the following timeline in your mind, it will help you not to worry about the settling-in period quite so much, as you will realise how extensive it may be:

One week – Decompression time at home.
After three weeks – Your dog should begin to realise that this home is more than a quick stopover, and you

may start to see signs of relaxing, playing and good habits forming. You may also start to see behaviours you weren't aware of, e.g. barking. If you are seeing any areas of concern, such as guarding, aggression or any habits that you are unsure how to deal with, this is a suitable time to reach out for tailored help before it escalates further.

After six weeks – You may feel that you are able to predict its reactions to certain people, or understand its likes, dislikes and fears. Your dog may also begin to feel bonded to you and your family.

After three months – It is usually possible to notice large changes, such as feeling that the dog knows who its family is and where its bed is, and what time it gets fed. You may see that concerns from early on are dissipating slowly but surely as the dog feels more reassured in its environment and home.

After six months – The dog should feel totally settled and like you have always had them, as part of the family.

I point all of this out as I think people generally have a very different time frame in their mind. And some dogs may be able to reach differing targets at differing points, but that will depend on their previous experiences, homes, relationships and the new home that they find themselves in. It will also be very telling as to how much the new home is a good fit for the dog and the person/family and whether a rescue was totally honest about the background and experiences of the dog you have taken on.

During this getting-to-know-you period, you should

be keeping a note of the things that motivate your new addition, the things they dislike, anything they are afraid of, areas that may need to be worked on. It can be really interesting to see how these things alter and change.

For example, when we first got our Great Dane, he used to go crazy when he saw birds – lunging, jumping, standing on his hind legs which, when a dog weighs 65 kilos and you are on the other end of the lead, can be a little much. So on our chart that we kept on our kitchen wall, birds were flagged as something we might need to address through some training work. However, after a few weeks of Fred being let off lead to run every day, twice a day for around an hour at a time, this concern over birds was removed from our list. He was exercised and stimulated enough through his walks that he couldn't care less about birds any more. Once exercise became predictable for him, when he realised it wasn't going to be taken away from him, that we would be taking him out every single day, come rain or shine, he could relax into it, and he could stop the worry over that which then affected other areas of his behaviour.

This early learning period with a rescue dog is really key, as it can enable you to stop something getting worse and to use the opportunity to teach new behaviours in a new home and in a new environment. This is the time to reach out and seek out a behaviourist to help you. Don't try to figure it out yourself, as by then you may have compounded the issue and made it a great deal worse, which will then mean it takes longer to iron out, if it can be ironed out.

WHAT IF IT ISN'T WORKING OUT?

This is sadly sometimes the case, if the match has not been done properly at the start. I once met up with a client who had been given a rescue dog by a charity, as he was a household name and the charity really wanted their name associated with his. However, within two days, he and I could both see this wasn't going to work. The dog he had been given was not what he needed, and really should never have gone to anyone living in London, so he had to drive it back to the rescue centre. This was heartbreaking, but it should not have happened in the first place, which is where your research comes in about choosing the right dog and not being pushed into a situation you don't feel 100% about. We then spent four months finding my client the right rescue dog; she and he lived a life of adventure until her dying day. Of course he had work to do with her, but it was all work he was capable of doing and loved doing.

I see the most mismatches coming from dogs who have been simply 'matched' via an online charity. The quick processes actually often backfire, as they haven't been done properly or in person. Do be aware of this. Anyone can say anything about a dog online, in the same way humans do on their dating profiles! If humans can lie about themselves, we can certainly lie about another species. Of course we want to help the dogs and remove them from the sad situations they are living in, but this must still be a match that is reciprocal for both human and dog.

CHAPTER SIX

Bringing Your New Puppy Home

A puppy needs to be coming home with you at eight weeks old, and there is absolutely no budging for me on this. It's non-negotiable. If you have a holiday booked, cancel it. If you have a job on that you need to do, don't get the puppy. Put simply, do not get your puppy at twelve weeks or fourteen weeks. The early weeks of socialising a puppy are absolutely essential for beginning to show your puppy what their new life will look like, sound like and smell like. This stage of development is critical and is about your puppy having many positive learning experiences for your life together. The right socialisation results in a confident, adaptable, happy dog. If you miss out on this period with your puppy, you will have lost out on crucial periods that will have an impact on their entire life with you. If you are going to do this properly, do it the right way.

Many people will tell you that you need a crate if you're bringing a puppy home. I'd say do not feel like you must buy one. They are not a must-have item. If you need to buy an item to restrict a puppy's movements, a baby gate or a pen can work just as well, if not better. It really depends so much on your lifestyle, your family make-up, your home and your dreams for the future. There are no hard and fast rules about selecting which option, as it really depends on your puppy's breeding and what they have experience of. It's rather like saying that 'swaddling works for every child' when we know this isn't the case. You do, however, need to be prepared to switch around between different options, depending on what your puppy needs and prefers. I find baby gates usually provide the most flexibility and I would recommend them for every home of any size. If your puppy is used to a crate from the breeders or rescue, or perhaps you have young children in the house, then a crate can be a good option. What I'm trying to say is that it's not as simple as buying one piece of equipment and it will solve all your problems.

That being said, there are a few items that I do recommend in preparation for bringing a dog home:

- A way to restrict your dog. A pen or baby gate is recommended. A baby gate is crucial if you have children in the home.
- A dog bed. It can be worth having more than one, in different rooms.
- Collar. Legally your dog must wear one with an ID tag on when out in public.
- A lead, but not an extendable one.
- Bowls. I prefer the heavy stoneware ones, that can't be picked up or moved.
- Treats. Don't go overboard to begin with: you don't want to upset stomachs, especially during the transition of moving from a breeder or rehoming centre.

Stick with very natural, meat-based options, e.g. turkey jerky or plain liver. Just start with a couple of options (see Chapter Nineteen on food and feeding).

- Food. Keep on what the breeder or rescue centre had them on for at least a week. Then look at the section within this book to decide what to begin to move your dog on to.

- Biological washing powder or liquid. To dilute in water to use on any accidents in the house.

- Toys. You need a number to figure out your dog's preferences, so don't go all out until you know a bit more about how your dog likes to play:
  - Tugger toy – something long that can be grabbed and tugged
  - Ball – not too heavy and not squeaky to begin with, as it can make them overexcited
  - Soft toy – to mouth and carry
  - Mental stimulation toy – that dispenses treats: an easy one, not one that you need a degree in physics to solve
  - Snuffle-mat-type toy or mat
  - Chew items – avoid the hardcore rubber bone types as few dogs I meet actually like those. Choose edible chew options instead.

- Old towel or puppy pads – for on your lap on the way home or in the crate in the car.

- A blanket that you can take home from the breeders or rescue centre, to provide some familiarity of scent for the first week or so.

- Insurance – buy the best one you can afford. The

cover that has lifetime cover for an illness or ailment is preferable, especially for a rescue dog with an unknown history.

- Harness or container for within the car for travel – there are many options out there, so you may need to figure out what will work best for your individual dog or puppy.
- Blankets – dogs often like to dig around in their bed and make themselves comfy, so even if their dog bed you have bought is beautiful, give them a blanket that they can ruffle around in and get themselves set up to sleep.
- Fencing and a gate – at your home and in your garden. Do not fool yourself that your dog won't get out of that tiny gap. Same with stairs and the gaps between the banister spindles for puppies. Get it all sorted before you bring your dog home.
- White-noise machine or app – these can be great for kids and dogs alike, as they provide a consistent noise which is preferable to the radio.

HOW TO DOG-PROOF YOUR HOME

Many people will think it can be excessive to go to a great deal of trouble about changing things in your home. I, however, have seen first hand the puppy who bit through a cable of a laptop and had a hole burned into his jaw, resulting in him not being able to eat for quite a number of days. With puppies, I see the knock-on effect of people who haven't proofed their space, resulting in not giving the dog any freedom, which then encourages a dependent dog.

A rehoming centre will question you regarding your garden, the fences, etc., but the home should also be a focus. Not the size of your house or how many bedrooms you have, but the prep work you have done to get your home ready to receive a new visitor while you are learning about each other. Slowly things can be reintroduced when you know more about your dog's likes, dislikes, whether they are a mischief-maker or a calmer companion.

External preparations

- If you have a garden, make sure your fences are high – six feet at least. I'd do even higher if you have a dog who can jump and is a great high-flyer! If you have a terrier type or street-dog rescue, you might want to look at making sure they also can't dig downwards, so make sure that under the fencing slats there is an actual wire wall. Bushes don't make a fence, they just make a more interesting hurdle to the outside world; they certainly won't contain a curious dog. I always remember my sister sending me a photo of her rescue Tibetan Terrier. They paid to have all their fences done. She looked out of her bedroom window, to find him doing a poo in the middle of next door's immaculate lawn! He had figured out how to jump on a chair, onto a table, onto a wall, onto a fence post and over it. He simply saw the fences as just another mental stimulation task to solve!
- If you have a pond in your garden, you will need

to be certain that your dog or puppy can either not get into it, or if they did that they can definitely get themselves out. You will need to make sure the pond has a ledge installed around the edges all the way around, and you will also need to make sure it has various ramps around it to ensure a dog can get itself out. The safest option is to fence the pond and make sure your dog or puppy cannot get in and drown. There have been some truly terrible tales of dogs that have done just this, and it is heartbreaking as the adventurous pup will have merely been exploring. Dogs don't understand the perception of depth, and the consequence of what could happen if they either have never done it before or if the previous times it was fun. I recently sourced a collar for a client who lives on a big country estate: the collar has an alarm and you keep the receiver in the house or with you, and if the collar on the dog enters the water, it will alert you immediately. This precaution was utilised as they have two ponds on their property. Ledges were also installed, as well as ramps and fencing. They took every preventative measure possible.

- Gates obviously vary in size and type, but if your hand can fit through a gap, chances are that the dog's snout could and a small dog could too. A client's dog was recently bitten in the face by another dog when it popped its nose through the gap of their front gate. Use something like chicken wire to make this impossible. And also make sure there are no gaps under the gates, where a dog can dig and create an escape bolthole, especially if a front gate goes directly on to a road. In the countryside you often see large gates to a property where the dogs just sit by them and then go manically crazy when anyone or anything walks by. Personally this isn't a behaviour I favour: the continual practice of that kind of squawking, barking or lunging does not bode well for a dog that is accepting of people and other dogs.

- There are various plants that can be dangerous to dogs, and often the bulbs are actually more dangerous than the actual plants themselves. There is a fairly long list of toxic plants for pets, so do your research online to figure out what you may or may not need to get rid of, or replant somewhere else out of harm's way.
- It can be worth considering if you want to create an allocated area for your dog to toilet within your garden: you can use a pen for a puppy or build an actual fenced area if you have the space. This can be particularly useful if you have children and would prefer to keep the dog's toileting habit away from where the kids play. You will need to do some work on teaching your dog an association with using that area. The best way to begin this is to start by using the first wee and poo of the morning, upon waking. Either carry a puppy or put your dog on a lead and walk them to the area you want them to use, and reward them when they go into it and toilet. It is worth having a contained area, big enough for the dog to walk around and get comfortable, as most dogs like to walk around a bit before they select where to squat or cock their leg. Slowly you can start to open the gate to the contained area and release your dog into it, knowing that they

need to go. Over the weeks, you can start to build up 'sending' your dog to the allocated area, and as soon as they have toileted, let them out. So it becomes a place to simply utilise and then be taken out of to play and explore. Do be patient, as this can take quite some time to build, and you will need to pay a great deal of attention to the surface they prefer. For example, a dog who is used to being in kennelling, or on the streets, will likely favour concrete, so do watch out for where they are going. If you are out on a dog walk and they go for a poo, pick it up and take it home with you, then place it in the allocated run you have created so it smells of them the next time they enter it.

- If you have a large garden (lucky you!) then it can be worth introducing the dog or puppy gradually, so as not to overwhelm them or to prevent them being overstimulated and not listening to you. You can buy pens that slot together with rods, which you can utilise as temporary fencing panels and join them all together. It can be a cheaper way of doing things while you figure out how your dog reacts to things.

- Fence chasing, boundary chasing, fence patrolling – however you want to describe it – can be something certain herding breeds can begin to do on fences where other dogs or people walk past. Once this has begun it can be incredibly difficult to change, but it can also create dogs that are very hard to manage due to the intense reinforcements that it can offer a dog. Be really aware of this if you have fences or perimeters where the public can walk past and make sure you begin working on teaching the right behaviour as a reaction to them passing by, instead of waiting to see what develops.

Internal proofing

- You can now buy rubber tubes that fit around cables and wires, and I'd wholeheartedly recommend these if you are bringing home a puppy. Cables fit perfectly into a puppy jaw, they have a lovely feeling of suppleness and a degree of tuggability. You only need to not be paying attention for a minute, or to leave the room, and the worst really could happen. So preventing it and tidying up the wires is truly the easiest and best option. If there are lamps or items you can remove, then that too is a good option. They won't need to go for ever but just while you are assessing chewing needs.
- When a puppy is learning where to toilet, there will be many accidents. So it is a good idea to remove rugs or items that you do not want to have to feel annoyed about if the inevitable happens. You also want to be giving your dog the freedom to explore and you cannot do that if there are things that you are worrying about them peeing on. You won't need to take them up for ever, but certainly while you are toilet-training it is worth removing them before you even bring them home. If you have slippery floor surfaces and you need rugs for the dog to be able to grip on to, then order cheaper, wipe-proof alternatives to use during the months of puppyhood where toileting accidents can happen.

- I would already have items like baby gates installed for when the puppy arrives, so it is all they ever know in their new environment. This is particularly important if you have other dogs or children in the home. Puppies are full on, intense, rambunctious bundles of curiosity and sometimes people and dogs need a break from them!

- Consider your coffee table, and what can easily be snaffled off it. Will they easily learn unwanted behaviour like jumping up on it to snatch things to get your attention? If so, clear the coffee table so you can ignore all their shenanigans around it, even if that involves climbing onto the top of it. Coffee tables can provide some solace for tired pups underneath them but where they still feel a part of things. If they do retreat, don't pull them out. Let them rest and sleep out of harm's way.

- House plants can provide amazing ways to play; digging in the soil, pulling at the leaves and stems and dragging of the pot are all very exciting options. In the early days I'd put them up high, or you can end up feeling like all you do is tell your puppy off, remove them from dangerous objects and try to distract them. You need to make your living space suitable for a puppy or new dog. All of these items can be reintroduced when their settling period is done and when the chewing, gnawing stages of puppyhood are firmly behind them.

- If your dog is going to be living with children, do consider where you keep the toys and the kind of access the dog will have to them. Very often people expect a dog to 'just know' what is theirs and what belongs to the children of the house. So when you are trying to teach these boundaries, cut your dog some slack and make it very clear where their items are. Make sure kids' toys like building blocks and other tiny pieces that can be swallowed by an inquisitive pup are well out of the way. Think about whether you would let a crawling baby who puts everything in their mouth around certain objects. If the answer is a certain 'no', then they aren't suitable for a dog or puppy either. Remember that a dog will mouth everything to understand its suitability for eating and to understand more about it. A swallowed object can cost thousands in veterinary fees to remove, when just tidying it away and out of reach would have saved all of the hassle. Again, this is why a baby gate is important, so that if your children are playing with toys that aren't suitable for a puppy or dog to be around, they can be safely contained while not posing any risk.

- I often hear people complain about dogs dragging their shoes away with them. Shoes are the perfect teething object. The rubber sole feels lovely to sink teeth into. Flip-flops with their foamy bottom are even better for tender gums. So if you don't want your dog to learn about shoes, store them away. Once again, this is a human object and a dog doesn't understand why it would be out of bounds when it can meet so many teething and chewing requirements. Don't fall into the trap of believing that a dog should just know not to touch it.

- Patio doors or bifold doors can lead to a great deal

of barking issues for dogs, as they essentially allow a dog to sit and reinforce any antisocial behaviours without you even being present. So while it can seem sweet to see the dog sitting watching the neighbour's cat tightrope-walking the trees above your fences, it will compound frustrated, predatory behaviours for many dogs, which will lead to frenzied barking. Prolonged barking at doors and out of windows can be easily prevented using tracing paper or similar taped to the glass to create a frosted appearance, so that the dog can't see out. Yes, it can feel annoying to have to do this but it will be more annoying to have a dog who for the next fifteen years of their life slowly works themselves into a full-on, manic, crazed dog barking at the garden. Although you may think the dog is enjoying 'guarding' the garden, the truth is this situation creates stress for a dog and makes it very hard for them to relax and switch off; it's not a relaxing state for a dog to live in for years on end. So do consider this when you are weighing up where to put your dog's bed, where to leave them to rest, where to put them when you leave the house, etc. A fox peering through the door at night can freak a dog out and create long-term associations that were preventable. A client had this with her Jack Russell Terrier, who got herself regularly worked up into such a frenzy that they ended up moving home, as the dog became 'on guard' every minute she was in the house. Guarding became an obsession as foxes, squirrels and cats came into the garden, on her watch, behind a glass barrier. Getting the dog to switch off and relax became impossible, which was so stressful that a move was the only solution.

SLEEPING ARRANGEMENTS

Many moons ago, letting a puppy 'cry it out' when you first brought it home used to be the done thing. It was believed that comforting a puppy was 'giving in' or would somehow create a needy dog. I wholeheartedly would tell you the exact opposite. I find that a dog who is comforted and reassured will adjust to its new home much more confidently in the long term. A young puppy that has just been separated from its mother and siblings will find being left to cry alone incredibly distressing, and it is likely to feel awful for you too.

The question you need to ask yourself about sleeping arrangements is what is going to work for you? Have you always wanted a dog who sleeps on the bed with you? Or is it important to you that your dog grows up to sleep in its own bed? The puppy doesn't have to start in your bed or its own, but it is a good idea to have an aim in mind. I would also point out that aim and real life can vary hugely once you actually start living with a dog.

If you would like to keep your puppy in your living-room-type area in the long term, it is worth considering for the first couple of weeks that someone should sleep on the sofa near them. You should be close by; the puppy shouldn't feel alone. You should be close enough to the puppy to offer a hand of reassurance should they need it. The puppy should not be distressed and howling, crying and yipping all night in the hope that you come back to them. You can have them in a crate next to the sofa, in a pen nearby, in a bed on the floor – the options are endless and it depends on what you are hoping for, so that judgement must be yours. The key is getting your dog to rest, to sleep and to feel safe. Those are the priorities.

If the idea of sleeping on your IKEA sofa for a few weeks fills you with dread (it would me, as our street is so noisy!), you may decide to sleep in your own bed with a pen or bed next to you on the floor, so you are there to scoop them up and take them for toilet breaks when they ask, and to offer a reassuring pat. Again, you are nearby, in sniffing and visual distance but without actually sleeping intertwined with each other!

Sleep is incredibly important for all of us, so you do need to set up an area that both you and your puppy are happy with. And you will also need to pay attention to the way your puppy naturally favours to sleep: the positions they lie in, whether they want to dangle off things as they sleep, or rest their heads on a ledge. Each dog will have its own sleeping preferences, and paying attention to these will help you set up a sleeping area that encourages rest. For instance, if your dog loves to have something to lean on when it sleeps, don't bother purchasing a flat bed or cushion, as they won't want to use it. Do look at all the pictures of your puppy sleeping that the breeder sent to you, as these will provide clues on your dog's ideal way to rest.

If you are going to use a crate for sleep, do make sure you set it up properly. All too often I see them set up like some kind of punishment cell, devoid of any joy! The crate should be like a puppy's own bedroom: it should offer comfort, solace and warmth. I would strongly suggest a properly fitting crate cover, not just a blanket draped over it, as kids can easily pull blankets off and disturb the puppy. I personally wouldn't worry about creating zones within the crate, such as an eating zone and a sleeping zone, I'd just make it all super-comfortable. If you have the space, then a pen with a crate or bed within it is ideal. That way, the pup can have the door to the crate open and access to the pen should they want to change positions, or have a wiggle around. This works so that should they need to toilet or get water or sleep on a cooler surface, they have a choice.

OVERTIREDNESS AND OVERSTIMULATION

Overtiredness is where a puppy has been awake for too long, has not slept enough or is struggling to get itself to sleep. Strange as it may seem, sleep doesn't come naturally to every dog, and as an owner you may have to help them rest. Most puppies are used to falling asleep with the help of their mother in the beginning, and then, when they start to be weaned, with the help and companionship of their littermates. That transfer of needs then gets put on to you, the new person in their life.

Look back at the photos or videos you got sent of your puppy with the breeder, or your dog in rescue, to look at how it was sleeping, who it was leaning on, how it sought comfort. These will be tell-tale signs of how you can transition your new pup to sleeping in your home.

Very often the behaviour of an overtired puppy goes south very quickly and we end up with what I call a baby shark. The baby shark creates havoc wherever it goes, biting everything. Owners end up with pinprick puncture wounds on their limbs, blood is drawn and emotions run very high.

I offer settling-in sessions to my clients and very often I arrive at people's homes to find them in tears or just not coping. It's often a result of an overtired puppy that needs some help in learning to rest and relax, so its owners can do the same.

Actively creating nap times, rests and breaks is really important in a pup's life. To give you an idea of the kind of sleep a puppy should have, an eight-week-old puppy should sleep eighteen hours per day. When you know that your puppy is tired, you can start to try to get them onto their bed. Begin to withdraw your attention, stop playing with them, give them items to chew on; this will assist in helping them to rest. You may find that they like to crawl under the sofa or the coffee table to collapse and sleep. You need to start identifying the habits that your dog indicates your pup is ready to rest.

Overstimulation will create the same manic behaviours as tiredness, but in this case it is usually due to inexperienced owners pushing a puppy too far – for example, with too much rough and tumble or chasing, which sends their body into adrenal overdrive. If you overstimulate your dog, its whole system gets fired up, and then you suddenly expect them to just switch off and stop because you've decided the game's over. A dog doesn't understand this, which is why we, as the carers, really need to pay attention to what overstimulates our own puppy, as it will differ from pup to pup, breed to breed. In the case of a Whippet or Irish Wolfhound puppy – breeds that are designed to use their eyes for everything – a great deal of movement could create overstimulation, e.g. walking along a busy road with cyclists whizzing past. Whereas for a Beagle, a picnic in the park could drive them crazy: being able to sniff out the buffet but not access it may result in a dog who is pulling like mad, won't listen to commands and isn't interested in the treats you have.

Children are also very good at whipping puppies and dogs into an overly stimulated frenzy and then screaming and crying when it goes wrong, so these interactions do need to be very heavily managed. And if you can't manage them, then the kids and dog should be on differing sides of a baby gate. Prevention is always better than cure when it comes to kids and dogs living harmoniously together.

If your puppy or dog is overstimulated, you can calm them down by . . .

- winding down any high-energy games or interactions
- giving them a change of scenery, e.g. the garden or front doorstep (somewhere calming!)
- providing chewing activities
- giving a licking activity
- taking them into the room where you would like them to settle, and removing your attention, e.g. sit on the sofa and read and allow them the time to get bored and settle
- lead them to a spot or a place where you know they

have chosen to rest before, e.g. a certain rug, a cushion, a chair
* make sure they have been to the loo, as this will help them to settle quicker.

PUPPY ROUTINES

When I had my children, I dreamed of discovering some kind of golden child-rearing path that would just make it all slot into place. Of course there wasn't one. Both of my children were very different from birth, and they had different needs. The same is true for puppies. You could take ten puppies from the same litter and their biological systems, toileting, etc. would each be their own. So with this in mind, I'm not going to offer you a set routine that every single puppy should follow.

What I can offer instead is more of a template that you can adapt around your puppy, depending on their breed, their personality, their character, your life and your surroundings. Because what may work for a pup living in a flat in the centre of London will be very different from what works for the family living rurally with a large expanse of land and a big roaring fireplace. It's not to say that one is better than the other, it is more about understanding that every dog and their set-up differs.

If your puppy can be awake for an hour at a time (which it should be from ten weeks onwards), I would be looking to break that hour into three twenty-minute sections:

0–20 mins – waking up, toilet trip outside, physical play and actual movement, walking, having fun outdoors, playing games inside.

20–40 mins – toilet break, making sure they're not getting too excited (or they won't go for a wee). This is a time for quieter activities, a potter in the garden, an observation walk, some brain games, training time, sitting on your front porch to observe the new surroundings.

40–60 mins – getting ready to go back to sleep, and offering help with this, such as chewing activities, licking activities in a pen, in their bed or crate (depending on what they like and will accept).

After 60 mins – aim to have the puppy back to sleep for between thirty and ninety minutes, time to make a cup of tea for yourself.

And then it's rinse and repeat.

The repetitive early days of puppy ownership can feel rather like Groundhog Day, and you should be prepared for this to go on for a few weeks as the puppy gets used to its new life. When I used to foster rescue pups, before I went to bed I'd prep puppy toys, make things and get items ready (ideas below) so that I had lots of options to pull from the next day, as looking after a puppy is incredibly tiring. Get ahead of yourself and make things easier for yourself and your pup.

Have ready:

- toilet- or kitchen-roll tubes with a treat inside
- carrots, frozen, for them to chew on
- cardboard boxes with holes punched into them, and treats wedged into the holes
- a pot of small treats to scatter feed on the floor, e.g. frozen peas
- chews suitable for dogs from twelve weeks of age.

TOILET-TRAINING

I sometimes hear that my clients have been told it should take just two weeks to toilet-train a puppy. I'm afraid this is hopelessly optimistic. To be absolutely honest, as a puppy owner, you need to factor in four to six months for toilet-training to be complete and reliable.

With a very young puppy, you need to be factoring in going outside together every thirty minutes. Which is a lot of getting up and down. By the time you get back into the house, put the kettle on and check your emails, it is time to go back outside again. It is a constant cycle of repetition for the first few weeks and then all of a sudden, you will realise that your dog has gone two whole days without an accident.

I am stating this because thousands of puppies get given up every year due to issues with toilet-training. People have unrealistic expectations. I was recently on a TV show with a woman who had a puppy for just twenty-one days before giving it up, as she didn't realise the toilet-training would be so hard, and nor did she expect that a puppy would need to poo and wee that much.

To be clear, I would expect an eight- to twelve-week-old puppy to need to toilet fifteen minutes after they have drunk any water. Usually there aren't huge amounts of time between it going in and coming out, so you do need to factor this in. Especially if you do not have direct access to a garden or a balcony. You need to account for toilet-training every day, every hour, even during the night. While your dog is young, you may need to be getting up three to four times a night to let them relieve themselves too. It isn't always the case, but it is best to be prepared that this is very likely.

If you live in an apartment block, do consider how you will manage this. Even if you are going to be training your puppy to toilet in the house, you still need to work out how this is going to be accomplished to create the desired habits you would like in the long term.

Generally speaking, I'm not a fan of puppy pads. I think they are a waste of money, detrimental to the environment and, ultimately, a company is profiting out of a product you do not need. I believe that using puppy pads runs the risk of essentially training your dog to see your home as their loo, when from day one we should be encouraging them to toilet in outdoor space, whether that is a balcony, a concrete courtyard, an acre of land or some AstroTurf. I believe we should begin as we mean to go on.

It may not always be easy to get your dog outside, but by using pads, you may need to toilet-train twice rather than once. Firstly the pup needs to be trained to go on the pads and then it has to be to trained again to get it off the pads and to use an outdoor environment.

If you simply don't have outdoor space, don't panic. You can still make a great deal of headway with toilet-training. You need to create a dedicated space that is used for toilet-training. Previously I've set these up in an en-suite bathroom or utility room, somewhere that becomes a space for a puppy to head to when it needs the loo. You will need to choose something for the puppy to pee on – and this will need to be something with a very different texture from your own floors, so the puppy can tell the difference, e.g. using AstroTurf with puppy pads underneath it, to soak up any liquids. You don't want a puppy to think it's fine to wee on any hard-floor surface, or on carpet. You can then begin to use the moment you see your pup start to head to the designated area to react and get your puppy outside to toilet instead. So you ultimately do achieve your long-term goal of having a dog who uses the outside to toilet.

HELP! MY PUPPY'S GONE FERAL!

Most of us have had those moments when our puppy runs around like crazy all over the house, ignoring commands, running into things, grabbing at your legs. In my experience, this often happens first thing in the morning and/ or when family members start arriving home in the evenings, e.g. after school. Many times, this is triggered by the puppy's overexcitement and excess energy, especially if they are too young to be going out on proper walks yet. The puppy is trying to find an output for that energy and it usually ends up being used by running laps of a house, or throwing themselves off sofas and into walls, grabbing at random items as they go.

On the flip side, anxiety can also trigger these outbursts, uncertainty and fear can also make a puppy want to run and, when contained, they don't have many options so they begin to lash out. This crazy running around may even be linked to a new visitor to the house, or someone coming in to do work and carrying tools in. New scents and objects being brought into the home can create all kinds of responses in a puppy that may lead to being over-stimulated.

A change of floor surface can help slow the manic running – for example, opening the back door so that the puppy or dog can get into the garden and run there instead. Usually trying to engage with them won't work, as the surge of adrenaline is too great and they need to get the energy out. Or they will have just become so overly stimulated that they cannot possibly concentrate or focus or listen. If it is too late to stop or prevent, it can be worth stepping on the other side of a baby gate and letting them get it out of their system, instead of trying to halt the behaviour or restrict them physically, which often then leads to owners being bitten as the puppy cannot cope with the restraint. This nipping or biting behaviour does not mean your dog is aggressive. They are trying to figure out the correct course of action, how to deal with their emotions and find a way to regulate themselves.

Rather than try to stop the feral moments as they're hap-pening, I find it's easier to prevent them in the first place by making sure the puppy has enough chewing activities, physical output, walks and plenty of sniffing time. In the worst-case scenario, where you miss all the signs and the puppy goes bonkers, sit on the sofa, tuck your feet up and let them get it all out. Just have a comfy bed ready for them to flop onto afterwards, as they'll be exhausted. Try to think back over what triggered the manic moment so that, the next day, you can adjust your routine or schedule to help them deal with the trigger more calmly. Never underestimate what a few decent walks can do, though, for managing a dog's anxiety or excitement.

If you find that these manic moments are triggered by people coming into the house, look at taking the dog out of the house to meet the visitors before they come in. Do a lap on the street first with the guest, walk and talk so as to get rid of the high emotion associated with these interactions. Look at toning down the excitement of visitors so that going crazy around new people doesn't become a habit for your puppy.

You may also have a puppy who pees out of anxiety when visitors arrive. This peeing usually isn't overexcitement, as many people attribute it to; it is more a feeling of being totally overwhelmed, which is why we do need to be careful about how we start teaching puppies to greet people at the front door. Instead of letting a puppy access the door, I would be getting people to enter while your your puppy is out of sight, behind a closed door or a baby gate. Wait until the new person has come in, taken off their jacket, got a drink and sat down before you introduce the puppy. That way, it will have had time to take in the sounds and smells of the visitor or visitors before it meets them.

WALKS

Anyone with a puppy will have heard the rule, usually from someone in the park, that 'You must only walk a puppy for five minutes for each month of their life, and no more, otherwise you will damage its development for life.' I would absolutely love to know who invented this rule, because it cannot be anyone who actually worked with dogs or puppies.

If your dog was four months old, by this theory you would only walk it or take it out for twenty minutes per day. Which would mean you just need to keep them indoors and entertained for the remaining twenty-three hours and forty minutes, which is absolutely bonkers to me!

I wholeheartedly encourage you to reject this myth, on the basis that no healthy dog should be exercised that little. This advice was originally given to those who had big or giant breeds, who grow very quickly and their bone plates are not yet fully developed or formed in puppyhood. However, for me this advice is still redundant, even for the big breeds, because if you are not socialising your dog, lead-walking them, taking them into the garden and playing with them outdoors, you will have many more issues on your hands than simply poor bone development.

No puppy should be run ragged, allowed to jump off things, or to be pummelled or pushed around by other dogs, or anything else that is going to jeopardise their bone structure or their physical health. However, a puppy *does* need to be out and about. They could be sitting at your feet at a café, walking beautifully on a lead very calmly and quietly, learning about travelling in the car, attending a hair appointment with you – all of this is a trip out of the house, and it is a chance to learn about and understand the big wide world. Being stuck in your home and only being allowed out for twenty minutes per day will not achieve any of this.

I see restricting walks in puppies also potentially causing a great deal of frustration for the humans in the house. And this can also lead to resentment about getting the dog, as it feels impossible to manage.

There are heaps of breeds who require a great deal of exercise even as a puppy. If you have ever tried to not exercise a Springer Spaniel for a day, you will know what I am talking about. They are literally like living with Tigger from *Winnie-the-Pooh*. They do not stop, they are always on the move, and they are full of beans, always. Rough play, boisterous play, running play with other dogs could very easily injure your puppy. They could damage their body and bones with this type of play, but there is far more to a walk or getting out of the house than meeting other dogs and I implore you to put the time and effort into doing this.

I understand that we have to be very cautious around bone development in puppies, especially in large breeds. If you do have a large breed, a giant breed, one who will grow quickly yet still be so physically undeveloped, you will need to exercise extra caution. Lumbering Labradors, gigantic Great Danes and boisterous St Bernards can be silly and not know how to control themselves. It is our role to prevent overexertion in these breeds as any damage to their developing bones could be long term. Doing walks in long grass, quiet places or on the street can all add socialisation and interest without risking their health.

I've found over many years of working with puppies that too much restriction when it comes to walks creates huge amounts of frustration and pent-up energy. A frustrated puppy jumping off a sofa onto a wooden floor, catapulting itself into a chair and then a table, will no doubt be more detrimental to its health than an additional calm walk around the block, or an extra sniffing excursion around the garden a few times a day.

What I have also come to realise over the years, and from living in London, is that many of the breeders who make this suggestion about restricting walks live within acres of land. They have big gardens, and some even have stables and paddocks. So their definition of a walk and leaving the premises is different from someone who lives in an apartment block or who has a minuscule courtyard patio. The time a puppy from a rural area with tons of space spends outside playing in the garden or pottering around the paddock isn't considered as exercise by these breeders; only the walking-on-the-lead bit.

But you do still need to be careful with a growing puppy. No puppy under twelve months of age should be running alongside a bike, or running alongside a human as they jog. A puppy's physical exertion needs to be managed carefully, depending on your breed. You can instead take your puppy to areas of long grass or woodland and encourage their natural sniffing behaviours. Sniffing, and interacting with an interesting environment, will calm and tire out a dog without lots of running around. Remember there are always other ways to get your dog out and about and moving without feeling like you are risking their health.

Ultimately it's your decision to make about how much you walk your puppy, but I'd hate for someone to be sitting at home feeling like they might have to rehome a dog, when a simple addition of a few more quiet excursions would have kept that dog in that family. If you are in doubt, seek help from a behaviourist who can provide suggestions of outlets, things to do and ways to exercise your particular dog.

If you're worried about overexerting your puppy, try these outings and exercises instead of a walk:

- Drive to the tip: lots of sniffs to explore once you get there
- Drive through a coffee/burger place, learning to hear voices, and seeing someone passing things through the window to you
- Sit on your doorstep to watch the world go by
- If you have a gated front garden, let them off lead to explore
- Play sniff games in the car boot or back seat, hiding a treat in the cushions or under blankets
- Lay out pieces of fabric, or create random surfaces for your dog to explore
- Visit a car park and have a slow meander around it
- Stand in the queue to get a coffee
- Visit a friend's garden, a new place to explore
- Visit the vet's surgery to hang out and then depart without actually seeing the vet (building in positive associations for the pup).

CHAPTER SEVEN

Socialising Your Puppy or Dog

Socialisation is one of the most important things we can do for our dog. It's how we introduce them to the world they will inhabit with us. For puppies, this is a developmental stage that has key points which need to be understood, as socialisation happens very early (often before a puppy has had its jabs). Older dogs also need socialisation to adapt to a new home, but for them this is about getting used to a new environment, rather than actual brain development.

Every family or individual taking on a puppy or dog should be writing their own list of socialisation exposures, as it will depend so much on where you live, your lifestyle and what you will need your dog to do in its everyday life. I often see these huge socialisation lists that clients are trying to tick off and work through, and they feel panicked, worried that they won't get through it all. So they are passing the puppy from pillar to post, taking them on huge adventures, exposing them to a gazillion overwhelming experiences and believing they are doing the right thing.

This is a good time to get out your list from Chapter

One and refer back to the kind of life your dog or puppy will be leading with you. Do they need to get used to children? Other pets? Public transport? Noisy traffic and busy streets? Tractors and horses? Every list should, and will, be different.

SOCIALISING PUPPIES

Socialisation is a period of time where a puppy should be given short exposures to people, situations and stimuli where nothing bad happens and no fear or anxiety is created. A well-socialised dog is calm and relaxed in most circumstances and can deal with unexpected people and events without panic or aggression.

'Primary socialisation' is the term used for everything a puppy encounters up until it leaves its mother, usually at eight weeks. 'Secondary socialisation' happens between eight and twelve weeks, once you have got the puppy home. Done well, socialisation is a gentle introduction to new experiences for your very young dog, and the process is going to be different for each family and each dog. If you live in a busy city, then your puppy is going to need to be introduced to things like traffic, pavements, buses and shops. If you live in the countryside, your dog will need exposure to cows, tractors, sheep, etc. So there is no one-size-fits-all socialisation experience that every puppy should go through, but there are some general principles that can be helpful to everyone.

A key thing to remember is that socialisation happens whether you are doing it consciously or not. A puppy is learning from the day it is born, learning about the world around it all the time. It's a good idea for us to at least have some intention around this process so that we can set our dog up for its future as part of your life.

I find that many of my clients have understood the definition of socialisation for a puppy as 'to take them to as many places, expose them to as many things, get them out and about and doing as much as we possibly can with every person, dog, child and adult we have ever known'. But this is often far too much for a puppy that is only a few weeks old. I think it's essential to remember that over-exposure, too much of something, will actually do as much damage as too little of something.

Slow it right down. If you live in a busy city, go and sit on your doorstep with your puppy on its lead and on your lap, or have them sitting on a blanket next to you. Sit yourself there for ten minutes and make a note of what you see. I'd imagine you might see bikes, cars, scooters, kids, people, dogs, cats, vans, shouting, laughing, high-vis vests, and hear the beeping of horns and much more. Your puppy can sit and observe this safely by your side, and when they have had enough, they can let you know by removing themselves. They might go back into the house, or they might curl up on your lap and go to sleep. They can make it very clear indeed how they're responding to the new experience. Let them show you their level of interest. Are they trying to get down the steps, to the end of the path, eager to get out and explore? Or are they happy with just sitting and watching? Neither is better than the other, but it is important to take socialisation at your puppy's pace.

When taking your puppy out and about, I find it can be

much better to carry your puppy in a bag than in your arms. This is because, when you carry it, every single person will want to stop you, will want to say hi to your pup. Some people won't restrain themselves or ask if they can touch the puppy, whereas in a bag, the exact opposite is true. A puppy can learn to watch and learn about the world, but also feel safe and secure that they don't need to feel intimidated, worried or anxious about people approaching them uninvited.

If you have a very confident, outgoing puppy already, they may not be anxious about people, they may actively search that attention out. If you have a more nervous, less confident dog, that kind of intense social contact with strangers at an early age can actually end up tipping them over the edge and creating a feeling of fear towards all people that will really start to raise its head from around five to ten months onwards.

For me, the biggest thing to remember is that puppy-hood is about preventing issues later on in the dog's life. You are trying to create positive associations and a good, interested reaction can only come if a puppy feels confident, relaxed and safe.

Socialising is about:
- brief, positive exposures to new things
- taking things slowly and gently
- remembering that you are sowing the seeds of the life you would like your dog to be involved with in the future
- understanding what your dog can do
- watching and learning, from a distance.

Socialising is not about:
- doing everything all at once
- overwhelming the puppy with constant stimulation
- allowing every man, woman, child and dog to touch and interact with your puppy – this will simply create fear
- trying to pack it all in
- making the dog fit into your life immediately – this takes time.

It may be helpful for me to list some of the unwanted behaviours I see in older dogs, which are created by the early socialisation that owners have done with their puppies, knowingly or unknowingly:

- A fear of people – because they were overhandled, have not had their boundaries respected and keep being picked up all the time.
- Fixation and total focus on other dogs – which can create reactivity, on-lead frustration, aggression or poor recall – usually created when, as a tiny puppy, they were taken up to every single dog you ever met and they were allowed to run over, go straight in and greet the dog. They were never taught how to walk past a dog or puppy, which is a crucial life skill.
- Dislike of certain stimuli, e.g. children – clients have told me that they sat outside school gates with a puppy and allowed all the children to come over and pet the dog. The puppy will feel overwhelmed and will start to generalise the children with this stressful, emotional state.

SOCIALISING A RESCUE DOG
OR AN OLDER DOG

When we take on an older dog, we obviously cannot go back in time to change, correct or switch around their life experiences. If their breeding, their socialisation, the way they were raised was not done positively and with consideration, then we can start to see the effects in their behaviour. Perhaps a dog was kept indoors by elderly relatives who adored it but never allowed it into the outside world, which would make the real world a scary place. You do have to take into consideration that a litter born in a rehoming centre may miss out on many socialisation opportunities, or, if raised well within a centre, could be exposed to many brilliant experiences – it all depends on the breeding of the litter, the efforts put in and the personalities of each dog.

Hopefully the rescue centre will have given you some advice about any particular issues to look out for, such as being anxious around new people. If something is flagged, my suggestion is to work with a dog behaviourist from day one to address issues rather than waiting a few months to see how things go.

You can use the socialisation advice above for puppies when socialising your rescue dog, but bear in mind that the primary socialisation period will be long past, and there may be some things that your dog will find hard to accept, no matter how much you work with them.

Again, you need to take things slowly. As mentioned

before, restrict visitors for the first few weeks, and introduce new people to the dog carefully and on neutral territory such as in the park or out on a walk.

I don't recommend throwing a new rescue dog into the deep end by instantly expecting it to go with you on all of your errands, or the school run. Give it time, and make sure you've factored in time for the dog to take regular breaks if it finds new environments overwhelming.

As the owner of a new rescue dog, I'd also suggest you limit the times you take the dog to places where you don't know how it will react, such as into a pub, or to watch a football match. Give it plenty of breaks, time out with a stress-relieving chew and lots of walks with sniffing – all of these will help a nervous rescue dog decompress from the stress of all the new experiences.

SOCIALISATION CATEGORIES

While I don't agree with hard and fast lists of socialisation, I do think it's helpful to break the socialisation period into smaller, more manageable categories. The reality is that you cannot possibly do it all, and even if you could, you would be exhausted, as would your puppy, and it would have defeated the entire purpose of socialisation.

Bear in mind that socialisation is where the puppy's breeding will really and truly come into play. If you choose well and bring home a confident, resilient, happy dog, you should not find there are huge shocks to the system as it gets used to its new environment.

When you're coming up with the socialisation list for

your puppy, there are a few broad categories you should consider, adapting each one to your circumstances.

People

In a busy city, socialisation could involve introducing a puppy or rescue dog to a lot of different people; for those in a village, it may be more about learning about the pace of life. I have found that some of the most common fears of puppies and dogs are around people wearing high-vis jackets, and hoodies that hide heads and faces. So it's a good idea to make sure your puppy encounters these early on, in a gentle manner. By this, I don't mean lots of people in hoodies need to come and try to touch the pup. Instead, you could just let your puppy see and observe people wearing hoodies, in a quiet situation where nothing frightening happens. You could wear a hoodie while you play a game at home, so long as your puppy is comfortable with this. Do think about who your dog is going to come into contact with the most; we want your dog to be able to believe that in general new people are good and nothing to be feared. Be careful about taking a young puppy into busy situations where there are a lot of people – a small puppy will be anxious around a lot of feet, and people grabbing at them uninvited will not instil confidence around strangers. Train stations and markets can be hard for a puppy to navigate.

Places and venues

If your dog is going to go to work with you, you need to consider exactly what that will involve, e.g. stairs, a lift, a studio environment, the kind of flooring it will encounter. These are all the areas that need some getting used to, not just the actual office itself, but what the process of going to work with you involves and what else goes with it, e.g. bright lighting, being on a really busy road, needing to be crated under a desk during meetings.

You may also want to be able to work up to taking your dog to a café or a pub with you. That work can begin far before you take them into an actual venue. You can be teaching and showing your puppy how to settle on the lead while attached to a chair or table at home. You can begin teaching your dog how to walk calmly on the lead so that you can carry a coffee in one hand and hold the lead in another. There are so many tiny things you can be starting to work on and build up to in a calm environment, before you even think about taking it out into the bigger, wider world.

Noises and sounds

I have clients who take their dogs into studios, on to the Tube, into very, very busy public places all the time, so a high tolerance of noise is key for their pups. Noise tolerance will be very much down to the breed you have and what work your breeder did with your puppy in their first eight weeks of life. A puppy raised in the home and used to the sounds of family life, from the whirr of the tumble dryer, the sound of the doorbell and hearing the radio playing every day will be far more likely to adjust than a puppy kept in a stable block in silence. Again, this may not be an issue if you are looking to take on a working Border Collie who will also live in kennelling on your working farm. However, for most people taking on a family pet, that is not their situation at all.

Vehicles and wheeled objects

Suitcases on wheels and skateboards can be some of the most common causes of fear and reactivity for many dogs. The rolling object, the noise, the unexpected movement and the sudden stop–start can feel far more intimidating to a dog than a car driving past. Imagine if that wheeled suitcase came in delivering their breakfast every day for a week, what would their association then be? Work to anticipate problems before they arise.

Again, think about what your dog's daily life may hold and what objects it may see regularly. If you are a photographer and your dog will be in a studio, familiarity with backdrops, wires, sets, photographic equipment, people coming and going, and smooth floor surfaces may be the most common components to studio life. This would be a very different socialisation need than a dog who will be with owners who work from home on computers most of the day. Those exposure levels differ accordingly.

Other animals and pets

If your dog is going to be coming to live in a home where you already have pets, this is an important factor in socialisation. In theory, a puppy being raised in a breeder's home where there are cats, for example, can seem like a good idea – they will be used to cats from a young age. However, if the breeder's puppies are allowed to chase the cat that they grow up with, it will be a hard habit to break once you get the puppy home. So it's not just about the animals a puppy has known, it is about their association with them. On the other hand, it isn't imperative for a puppy to have grown up with them to be able to accept other animals; it is more about the breeding of the dog and its natural confidence to be approachable and accepting.

At home

In order to get your dog used to your home, you need to look at what their life looked like at the breeder's, or what you know of their previous homes if you are bringing home a rescue dog.

If your rescue dog has only ever lived in kennels, you can be certain that the acclimatisation to a home situation could take quite a while. They will need to learn to understand the noises and how things like washing machines and hoovers work and function. They may be unused to things that won't have occurred to you, such as stairs, doorways or different floor surfaces. The process of getting them used to this new environment will depend on how long they have been kennelled, whether they were born and raised in kennels or if that is the only set-up they know. Very often we like to feel like we have 'saved the dog' and want to give them everything that they ever missed out on. However, we do have to remember that for a dog who has never been shown love, or not had a great deal of human interaction or comfort, our approaches may actually be terrifying. A rescue dog does not necessarily want or need to be smothered with love – give it space and time to approach you first.

When we bring a puppy home, we often make assumptions that they will understand that shoes aren't for chewing on, or that dressing-gown cords aren't tug toys, but why should they know that? Those items belong in a human world and are often left out in front of the puppy, who just sees something to play with. Rather than get annoyed, just keep these things out of the way.

The same is true of a rescue dog who has perhaps only lived with an elderly owner, living within a small world of being cocooned indoors. We cannot expect that they will be ready or able to make their world bigger. It will depend on their breed, their age and their natural personality. It is important to understand a rescue dog's circumstances before committing to taking that dog on, as some behaviours may be immovable.

PARK LIFE

It can be tempting to make going to the park the main focus of your outings with your dog, especially with a young puppy. Other dogs become a real target for your attention, owners actively scanning the horizon for any other dog owners and heading over to them at a pace so as not to miss the opportunity of introducing their dogs for fun and games.

I recognise this instinct to entertain your dog, but the real purpose of these walks should be getting your dog used to the outdoor environment, them learning to toilet there and learning how to be exercised and play with you in an outdoor situation. It's important for your puppy that the focus on you carries on outside, that other dogs can be great but that ultimately you are where the fun is at.

If your dog just sees you in the role of chauffeur to the park, who doesn't play or doesn't dish out treats, it's no wonder that it will run off to play with other dogs, who it sees as more fun! Walks should be about building fun, games and playtime between you and your dog, and this means limiting the amount of time you expose your dog to, and allow play with, other dogs.

You should be able to see your dog/puppy at all times – and not let it run out of sight. Use a five- to eight-metre long line if you need to, so that they cannot just disappear. I have seen a dog run out of a park, cause a car accident in which it got hit, and then return to its owner who was none the wiser. It could have been a lot worse for both dog and driver. So please keep your dog, and everyone else, safe.

Focus on finding older, calmer dogs that your dog can learn to walk alongside, not bother and to chill out with. You may find a couple of dogs that your dog enjoys playing with, and that is fine, in small doses. My rule of thumb is that dog to dog interactions should make up 10 per cent of the walk you are on, so long as that play does not spill into overstimulation which can lead to aggressive play.

As much as your dog is learning from you, it is also watching and learning from other dogs. So as long as the dogs you spend time with are good example-setters, it can also be incredibly useful. By a good example-setter, I mean an older dog who is calm, confident, non-aggressive and not overly playful, a dog who listens to commands and doesn't go running up to other dogs all the time. Allowing your dog to watch what's going on in the park from several metres away, without yet interacting, can be a great way to give a puppy a glimpse into life at the park.

I suggest that, before you take the dog to the park, you should think about the parks that you use and rate them in order of difficulty or distraction. By this I mean all of the many people and things your dog will encounter at each. Park life is not just about dogs, but also about human visitors who use those shared spaces: cyclists, joggers, buggies, kids on scooters, people sharing food, listening to music, doing exercise. With a puppy or a rescue dog, you want to begin their outdoor socialisation somewhere easy and with as few distractions as possible. You must not begin at the hardest, most full parks. You might spend months working up to that. And even then, you may only visit those sporadically.

It can be a good idea to take a nervous dog out early in

the morning, to avoid too much distraction. This allows you to gauge where your dog's boundaries lie and what, if anything, is too much for them.

All of this new sensory information can be overwhelming for a puppy, so let your dog watch from a distance and learn from what it sees. Young puppies that get overwhelmed by stimulus will often sit down, seemingly out of nowhere. Please don't drag your puppy and force it to walk in these moments, and don't let other dogs run up to it. Just allow your puppy to take everything in until it feels ready to walk again. I call this 'information gathering' and it's incredibly important at various stages through puppyhood, not just in the secondary socialisation period when you bring them home at eight weeks.

EVERYONE HAS AN OPINION!

As a new dog owner, you will soon start to realise that everyone and their mother has an opinion on your puppy and how you should or should not be doing things! The conflicting advice can feel overwhelming as you don't want to offend well-meaning people whom you meet on your walks or in the park, but you do also have to remember that what worked for a stranger's dog may not work for yours.

Dog owners often feel anxious about offending total strangers, but if you genuinely feel uncomfortable around another dog or dog owner, make your excuses and disappear into the sunset. So many issues can begin in puppyhood that I do think you need to listen to your gut, you need to know your dog and you know what feels right, and if you are unsure or it doesn't feel clear, then seek out a knowledgeable behaviourist's opinion rather than someone you met on a dog walk.

If your dog is fearful, or if your dog doesn't like another dog doing something, walk away. You do not need to stand there so your dog can get used to it. I don't like being slapped around the face, and having it done to me every day will not make me like it more.

Signs that your dog may be struggling within a social setting:

- barking at you or other dogs
- scrabbling at your legs to be picked up
- chasing: it isn't always done in fun – it can be a dog trying to get away
- running between and into your legs
- your dog constantly under siege from other dogs
- chewing on the lead
- not interacting but head down sniffing, wanting to get away.

Your dog may keep asking to be picked up in certain situations it finds frightening, often by trying to climb up your legs, or clinging to your legs. Other owners may tell you to keep the dog on the ground and ignore them, to just 'Let the dogs sort it out between themselves'. Please, please do not ignore your dog, and what they are asking for. Trust, and the bond you have with your dog, is the most important thing to be cementing. Do pick up your dog if they are requesting this. Many breeds, like

Whippets, Italian Greyhounds and Daxies, will scrabble at your legs in social situations. Don't ignore this, as there may be consequences. A client of mine's Italian Greyhound used to run out of the park every time he was scared as an adult, because as a puppy he had scrabbled at his owner, asking for help and to be picked up, but the owner had felt it was rude to do this in front of other dog owners. So the dog eventually changed its tactic. It stopped asking for help and just ran away, far more dangerous in every situation than a simple pick-up.

Some clients I know have been chastised by another owner for picking their dog up because 'It will make my dog jump up to get your dog'. The answer is simple: teach your dog to not stalk other dogs, teach your dog to not jump up at other owners. That is the responsibility of the dog owner, not of the person whose dog is being chased.

Lastly, before you take anyone else's advice on board, look at the situation you find yourself in, and look at the other person's dog. Is it well mannered, is it well behaved, is it being listened to, is mutual respect being shown, do you feel comfortable, does any of either the dog's or its owner's behaviour make you feel uncomfortable? Use these questions within your own head to decide whether or not you follow their advice.

CHAPTER EIGHT

Neutering and Spaying

One piece of advice that everyone in the park has strong opinions on is when to neuter or spay your dog. And I have to say I have strong opinions too. Many vets advise you to do this at six months of age, which I personally feel is too early unless there is a particular medical issue that makes it necessary.

The hormones in our dogs' bodies have specific functions, helping to regulate the body, particularly as a dog matures. These hormones can also have an effect on a dog's physical conditions, their behaviour, their mental capacities and the way they live their life.

Every dog's hormones, just like every human's, will be different, but the following list will give you an idea of the kinds of areas that hormones can affect in your pet:

- bone development
- scavenging behaviours
- aggression
- reactivity
- lack of confidence

- phantom pregnancies
- cruciate ligament ruptures
- hip dysplasia.

This list is certainly not exhaustive, but it serves more to illustrate the role of hormones on a dog's body. We should not disregard the impact of hormones on the health and behaviour of our dogs. I am not saying that you should *not* neuter or spay your dog, but in my opinion if this needs to be done then it should not happen before a dog has reached maturity.

I feel very saddened to find out that in the USA some breeders have started neutering at birth. This is just an awful thing to be doing for so many reasons. Most vets will recommend these processes be carried out well before a dog has stopped growing, before they have physically or sexually matured. I cannot and will not provide a rule of thumb for when a dog should be neutered or spayed, as I take each dog case by case. For most dogs living in dog-dense areas, it may need to be something that needs to be addressed if unwelcome behaviour is being experienced or it is disrupting a dog's ability to learn, focus and get on with their life. We had to take this decision with a lovely eighteen-month-old Weimaraner client of mine, whose dog was left entire to make sure all growth was complete, but other male dogs took an aversion to him and would start picking a fight with him. So he was neutered as we could not risk this becoming a constant feature of every dog walk and encounter. We have all heard the stories of the dog who crossed a road to get to a bitch in season and got hit by a car. None of us want those things to take place if we can prevent it.

It is also worth pointing out that keeping a male entire because you simply don't like the idea of 'cutting its balls off' is not a valid reason to leave them intact. Leaving a dog with a sexual desire and ability, and for it to not be fulfilled, throws up all kinds of other arguments in terms of fairness, kindness and a dog being able to lead a fulfilled life.

It is important to note that if you have an aggressive or reactive dog, neutering them will not magically solve the problem. But it will prevent that dog from ever mating and passing on the issues to further generations of dogs, so I would suggest it should most definitely be done.

I would always recommend that you discuss the appropriate time to neuter or spay with your dog behaviourist. They should know your dog well and be able to offer insight into the right time for your dog. For a bitch, I would never recommend spaying before a first season, unless there are medical reasons that overshadow waiting. None of us, including your vet, has a crystal ball, so none of us can predict when a bitch will come into season, and for me it is far too risky to spay before she has a season as, when they come to the operating table, they may well find the process has begun and now it has been disrupted.

We are starting to see more vets prescribing chemical castration, which is where a male is chemically injected to prohibit the hormones. I can't say I'm a big fan of this type of chemical treatment for long-term use, when a simple operation could be carried out. In my opinion there would need to be very good reasons to take this option, and I would hope the behaviourist, the vet and nutritionist were all working together to look at the bigger picture of behaviour that was trying to be solved.

I have used temporary chemical castration with clients who were unsure about having their dogs castrated, but only as a short-term option.

You may be hesitant to have your dog spayed or neutered because you are considering breeding from them. In order to decide whether your dog should be bred, you need to really sit down and invest the time to look at and answer the questions honestly.

- For what reason do you want to breed? You need to have a seriously good reason to bring yet another litter of dogs into this world. So your reason should be top notch.
- What makes you feel like your dog would contribute favourably to the world? What addition would they make to people's lives?
- What attributes make him worthy of being bred? Their personality needs to be one that you feel you would want others to benefit from.
- Can you afford to health-test both sire and bitch? As this should and must be done.
- Does the dog have excellent physical conformation and proven health? Not just looking at the breeding standard, but looking at their ability to be a dog, to function as a dog, to be exercised, to be free from deformities.
- Is the temperament of the dog you are considering absolutely excellent? There should be no 'ifs' or 'buts'. You should categorically feel confident in the temperament of the dogs you are considering mating.
- What are you trying to produce in the breeding of

your dog? Is it to keep a family line going as you adore
your dog so much? Or is it simply to make money?

- What is the main motivation behind wanting to breed
your dog? I always try to determine and understand
this when I talk to a breeder. It impacts the outcome
of the entire litter and the dog you end up living with.

The point of all of these questions is to draw your attention to the amount of dogs we have entering the world,
whose breeder has not sat and thought about any of this.
They have simply considered the cash to be made.

If you were ever going to consider breeding your dog,
you should wholeheartedly, without a doubt, know that
your dog is the most wonderful role model of how that
breed or crossbreed could turn out. You should know
that you have bred for the best health possible, for the
loveliest personality, unless you are breeding for a particular
working purpose where their working skill has to be
factored in too.

Having seen the heartbreaking impact of poor breeding
too many times, I have come to the conclusion that most
people should not be breeding their dogs. Please take this
decision very seriously if it's something you're considering.

PART THREE

What Your Dog Wants You to Know

CHAPTER NINE

What Your Dog Wants You to Know
about Creating an Incredible Dog

When I think of the foundation of having an incredible dog, I don't mean an agility champion or a winner at Crufts, I mean an incredible best friend, companion and family member. In my experience there are three key principles that you need to have in mind at all times when you are trying to teach and train your dog:

Eye contact
Motivators
Relationship

How many times have you looked at your dog, or puppy, and wished you knew what it was thinking? I can't help you become a canine mind-reader, but after years of learning, observing and working with hundreds of different breeds and thousands of different dogs, I have picked up a lot of information that can help you understand what your dog wants you to know.

For me, this whole chapter could go on and on, but I've attempted to condense it to pinpoint the areas that I feel are the most immediately actionable for you as a dog owner. Nobody wants to feel like their 'to do' list is being added to and extended indefinitely.

I think it is also important to remind ourselves that none of us sets out to do things incorrectly with our dogs. It's no one's intention to do things badly as a dog owner. We do have to remember that living with a dog is living with a different species. You both need to figure out how the other one operates, what makes them tick and how to make things work in the best way possible. It takes time and patience, but it can result in one of the most rewarding relationships of your life.

Although I will teach you the principles of understanding your dog, you will still need to work out the exact intricacies of your own dog's behaviour. Each dog is different, and you are the person who observes your dog the most, so learning the body language and behavioural 'tells' of your own dog will be a lifelong process.

EYE CONTACT

Dogs are natural observers. They are giving off tiny movements and physical signifiers all day, every day. So, for them, giving eye contact and using it as a way to communicate is completely natural. For instance, if you have ever observed a puppy on a busy road, you will have seen its eyes darting around, noticing, following and taking in. It is we humans who feel confused by eye contact with our dogs, lack experience in using it or simply don't understand the extraordinary difference good eye contact can create in the relationship between an individual and their dog.

For me, eye contact is the unspoken language between you and your dog. When you understand it, and how to use it, it can help your relationship blossom.

If you have recently brought home a puppy, you may notice how much it is looking at you. It is constantly assessing your reactions, asking permission, checking in regarding a situation, asking for help, or just making sure you are there and with them. An older dog may use eye contact to express its needs – the hard stare that tells an owner they're late to serve up a dog's supper will be familiar to most of us. Or the pointed look from a toy to you and back to the toy again to get you to play a game. Eye contact helps you feel like you and your dog are understanding each other.

It may sound obvious, but eye contact is a sign that you are paying attention to your dog, and attention should be mutual. A dog that knows you are attuned to it, and checking in on it visually, is also less likely to ignore you and run off to something more interesting. Letting your dog see that you are checking in with it as much as it is checking in with you builds a really important bond for life. And if you're often doing something interesting to your dog, such as offering food or attention or toys, it will want to check in on you all the more.

If you teach a dog to use eye contact to gain your attention, then you can start to use this silent communication for when a dog feels uncomfortable, to release them to play, to know if they would like another dog to leave them alone, to get them out of situations they dislike. Establishing this mutual trust and connection between you and your dog leads to another end result – less reactivity in your dog, less need for aggression, less need to fight or confront dogs, people or kids that make them worried or unsure. All in all, eye contact is a winner for both of you.

If you live with a blind dog, I don't want you to think that I am excluding you from this section. I'm certainly not; a blind dog can still check in with you and seek out your attention or permission or help, but it just won't happen via their eyes. They will still turn to you, and they will still hunt you out, but you will need to make the reward clearer to them and that will usually come via scenting or touch.

My deaf Bulldog, Cookie, used to adore it when I praised her by clapping, using my hands like little starfish, and wiggling away. She would wiggle in response, with her back end going crazy. She couldn't hear me but it was probably one of the experiences that early on highlighted to me the power of eye contact.

I love these three simple exercises for building better eye contact with your pup. These are just the starting points, but a great way to begin the work with your puppy or your dog. Do not run before you can walk and do not make it too tricky for either you or your pup. Each exercise needs to be built up slowly. You can start to practise each time you are waiting for the kettle to boil – I would rather you did shorter sessions than trying to draw it out for too long.

It is also worth bearing in mind that there are two purposes to these games. One is to teach eye contact and the other is for your puppy or dog to start realising what an ace person you are to hang about with.

I don't feel it is ever too late to work on improving eye contact with your dog. It is obviously easier if you capitalise on it with a puppy, but if you haven't then there is still time.

1. Treat eye-contact exercise

Start using a treat packet of low-ish value treats. By low value I mean some kind of food that your dog is interested in but isn't going to lose their mind over, or try to grab, otherwise you are making it too distracting for them right from the beginning. You can try a small dry biscuit, or similar, to begin with.

The purpose of this exercise is to introduce a distraction (food) and for your dog to understand that it gets the food when you get given eye contact. It is a win–win situation for everyone involved! We want your dog to start to learn that eye contact is the gatekeeper to everything good. And this exercise is incredibly easy to do and a joy for a dog to learn.

STAGE ONE

Open the treat packet with your dog next to you or near you and simply make a big deal about noisily opening the packet, giving them a couple of treats, then closing the packet and putting it away – you don't need to talk! Do this a couple more times during the day, when your dog isn't particularly expecting to get fed.

STAGE TWO

Later on in the day, sit on a chair or, if you have a tiny dog, kneel on the floor. Then open the treat packet, hold the packet against your stomach at belly-button level, placing a treat between your fingers but keeping the treat within the packet. Your dog should stand or sit next to you. (Don't ask them to sit or similar; don't ask them to do anything in fact.) Let them stare at the packet. Because you have prepped them earlier, they know a treat should be coming. Keep your fingers with the treat between them inside the packet, and keep your eyes focused on your dog's face and eyes. Don't call the dog or use any distractions to tempt him. Instead, wait for him to either (a) look away from the packet and perhaps at the floor or (b) look up at you to see what is taking you so long. As soon as he does either, you insert a word. I use 'yes' and then reward immediately with the treat. If you use a clicker, you could of course use this instead of a word to mark the eye contact.

STAGE THREE

The intention is to teach your dog to look at *you* in order to get the treat, rather than at the food or the packet. They need to be actively selecting to look away from the distracting treat packet.

If your dog did option (a), then for the first five or six times you repeat any time they look away from the treat packet, and you may not get any eye contact initially. But we still reward the fact that they have taken their eyes off the treat packet. It isn't the ideal thing we are working towards but it is still eye-contact movement. After your dog starts using the 'look away' as their default behaviour from the treat packet, I'd like you to hesitate and don't reward them. Wait for them to try another behaviour, which could be the tiniest, quickest eye flicker towards you, then say 'yes' and reward.

You can then start to build on this after a number of repetitions, so that the eye flickers towards you turn into longer glances. And then the glances will turn into head turns and your eyes will meet! Just go slowly with it and don't get frustrated. Don't be tempted to try and speed things along by calling your dog's name or making noises to get them to look. The whole point is that your dog is actively selecting to look away from the distraction without you asking or telling them; this is a free choice that we are going to capture.

Dogs from breeds that were bred to work alone, use their nose or be independent can take a while getting to grips with this exercise. We are teaching them to go against their years of breeding, their gene pool and what they are designed to do. A Patterdale Terrier isn't bred to stop, check in, make eyes and then go to work; the vermin it's meant to catch would be long gone by then! So there may be a reason why it's taking a bit longer to teach your dog this eye contact.

With some rescue dogs or older dogs, it may be that you have spent years ignoring their eye contact as you didn't realise it was important. This is OK too. Now is the time to begin rectifying it. Just keep practising the behaviour for option (a) above. We can work with disconnection and develop it into eye contact.

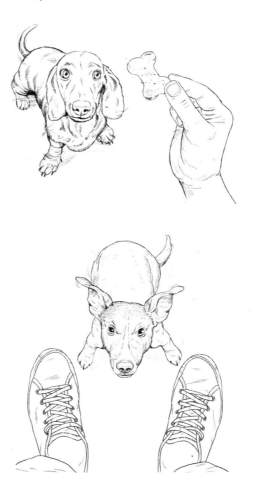

Reward the moment when the eye contact moves from the treat to you

2. Long line eye-contact exercise

This is a super-simple exercise, and all you will need is a five- to eight-metre long line. A long line is not the same as an extendable lead. A long line is a set length of lead, usually around five metres, that is attached to a harness (so not too much pressure is placed on the dog's neck) in order to start giving them a little bit of freedom while you keep hold of the other end.

STEP ONE

Take your dog or puppy to a place that is very, very low in distractions (what is considered distracting will differ from dog to dog of course). Ideally do this exercise somewhere fairly empty of people and other dogs. If you only have busy places to exercise your dog, try to go very early in the morning, so that it is quiet. If you have a really big garden, you can do this there.

Once you have selected your quiet place, walk around for a few minutes with your dog on the long line. Let them do their thing – sniff, walk, pee, whatever it is that takes their fancy. Don't ask anything of them for the first five minutes. Try not to talk to your dog either; keep it quiet.

STEP TWO

Then, when your dog is relatively close to you and on the long line, just stop walking. Wait for them to turn around to 'check in' on what is going on. At this point your dog won't be checking in with *you*, it will merely be checking in to see what on earth is going on and why there appears to be a stop happening.

As soon as they turn to check in, you say 'yes' or whatever word you have chosen as your cue and you throw the treat to where they are standing. This is not a recall game, this is a check-in, eye-contact game, so do not be tempted to ask for anything else from your dog at this point. It's all about the eyes. If you try to make the exercise too complicated, your dog will give up and not bother engaging. We don't want them to lose interest in the game before you have even really got started.

REPEAT

Once they have snaffled the treat, you just carry on walking, using a cue like 'let's go', allowing your dog to sniff and explore. Occasionally just stop without warning or cue. Once the dog stops and turns around to check in on you, reward as you did before.

Some dogs may only stop because they got to the end of the long line and they had no other choice than to turn and discover why. This isn't ideal because it shows they aren't listening out for your footsteps, or keeping a track on what you are doing; they are simply waiting until their lead gets tugged and then they stop. It is still better than no check-in! Your task here is to build up their check-ins until they are regularly, and voluntarily, stopping what they're doing to check where you are.

STEP THREE

Once you've established eye contact with the long lead, it's time to try without. Let your dog off its lead and reward voluntary check-ins (i.e. when you haven't called them or given another cue to pay attention). So, for example, if they are having a snuffle in long grass and they pop their head up to look for you, use your cue word 'yes' and throw a treat to them in the grass right where they're standing.

If you are walking them off lead and you are both merrily walking and your dog is up front ahead of you, occasionally just stop, without alerting them that you are stopping. Wait to see how many seconds it takes for them to be aware you have stopped and for them to check in with you (which you must then reward).

When I practise this step with dogs that I'm training, I count the seconds it takes at the beginning, to track the improvement later down the line. The sooner they notice you've stopped, the better. If you don't feel that the improvement is decent enough and moving along as fast as you would like, really take a look at the level of distractions where you are walking the dog. Are you expecting too much from them in a busy environment? Also consider if your dog is getting enough daily exercise. If not, it will prove so much harder to improve their focus because their excitement at being out of the house takes over. Equally, if you have a dog who just adores using their nose, you will need to select a location where the great opportunities for sniffing aren't overwhelming, or else you are making it too hard for your dog.

3. Toy eye-contact exercise

You will need to pick a toy that your dog is motivated by but not one that makes them overly jumpy or bitey. Just as in the first exercise, they need to be interested but not too excited.

STEP ONE

Begin a low-energy floor-based game with the toy, such as simply holding on to the toy and seeing if your dog is showing an interest in putting it in their mouth or putting a paw on top of it. This is about making sure the dog is interested in interacting with the item you have chosen. If it's not engaged, pick a toy it likes better.

STEP TWO

Then, while sitting on the ground, so it's easy for you to really watch your dog's face, cover the toy with your hands so it can't be seen or played with. Let your dog start looking for the toy. Some dogs may start to jump up or claw at your hand. Ideally I want you to ignore this and sit and wait. At some point they will usually sit and stare at the toy within your hands. As soon as you get a flicker of the eye contact towards you, reward with the toy immediately.

STEP THREE

You can then start to build on these, so that the flicker becomes a longer glance and then you reward. We do have to go very slowly, making sure to slowly build on the duration of the game – the aim is that it isn't always an instant reward with the toy, but equally we want to avoid making it so tricky that they get annoyed or bored and stop giving you the eye contact.

MOTIVATORS

Motivators are the things that your dog likes or loves to do. These vary from dog to dog, from food to toys, to games, to sniffing, to certain parks, to certain people and much more besides. I often ask clients to come up with a list of motivators for their dog – and once you start paying attention to this you may notice new ones that had passed you by.

My clients often joke that the primary motivator for their dog is cheese, and I've got to admit that I've yet to meet the dog that isn't interested in a piece of Cheddar. However, we can't always use high-value treats like exciting foods, so it is preferable to have other options open to us too.

I once came home to find our Great Dane, Fred, lounging on his back on the sofa as my husband fed him warm, fresh cuts of roast beef. I'm all for sharing the love, but let's reserve the most motivating treats (warm roast beef) for when we actually need them!

We need to find all kinds of motivators to keep our dogs engaged and interested – just like us, a dog will have likes and dislikes, joys and fears. It's worth noting that a dog's motivations will dip and change all the time, depending on the environment, the context and distractions. This can be why people are confused that their dog loved the ball at the beginning of a walk but couldn't care less about it by the end.

First off, let's take a look at your dog individually, as motivators vary enormously. If you have multiple dogs, you will need to do this for each of your dogs separately. Multi-dog households are wonderful if you have the time and space. However, we still need to recognise that, even if you have dogs of the same breed, individual personality and character play a huge role in motivation, as do the dog's life experiences, socialisation and so much more.

When you have more than one dog, it is important to carve out time for each dog independently, depending on their motivators. I'm currently working with two rescue dogs from abroad, who are polar opposites. Although they are both rescue dogs from a similar part of the world, and a similar breed, the male was abused and is terrified of strangers, while the female dog loves people. I have given the owners permission to leave the male dog at home while they take the female out to the local market and park and for a coffee. That busy situation with people around is motivating and enjoyable for the female dog, but absolutely terrifying for the male. So you can see that even with dogs from the same household, we can't just lump them into the same category and expect the same things to work.

I suggest you write a list of the motivators that are

specific to your dog or dogs. These can vary enormously, so, to give you an example, here is a list I have created for my dog Pip. He is a seven-year-old rescue boy who, at the time of writing, we have had in our lives for one year.

Pip's motivations in life:

- his people (my family)
- food – meaty treats especially
- sniffing
- a cricket ball
- my kids
- not being told off (this comes from his life before us: he was scolded heavily and is now fearful of being told off)
- playful dogs
- avoiding water
- snuggling up in his bed in our bedroom
- treat-dispensing toys (he has quite a few)
- 'find it' games to be played together
- tugging games – he is just learning about these, and enjoying them, so I plan to build on these as a motivator.

Within this list, you will see that a few categories emerge:

- Food
- Toys
- Games/Play
- Avoiding certain things
- Affection and touch.

Focusing on these categories will be a great starting point for you to explore with your own dog, to help work out what motivates it most.

As you can see from Pip's list, I have quite a few motivators to utilise. The next step is understanding when to use them. Here's an example. Pip loves to fetch and bring back a hard red cricket ball if my son is playing with it in an open green space like a field or a park. However, if I use that same ball in our tiny garden, the ball can hit a wall and bounce off, which Pip doesn't like. So in the situation of our garden, trying to motivate him with the red cricket ball would be a non-starter.

The same is true with regard to other dogs. Pip loves other dogs, and is very sociable and very gentle with his greetings and play. At the beginning of a walk he is desperate to greet each dog he sees, so I may use games and high-value treats to keep him close by and not distracted. At the end of an hour-and-a-half walk, he has lost interest in saying hello to every dog, so I barely need to worry or motivate him as he is now more tired and worn out. His motivation at the end of the walk is that we are all together and he is happily plodding back to the car with his gang by his side. And he knows he is coming home with us, his family: this is a huge motivator for him.

I do feel it is also worth pointing out here that, sadly, for some rescue dogs who haven't had the greatest experiences or perhaps have had difficulties, their motivations can also include some avoidance of certain things.

The male rescue dog I mentioned earlier was from Italy, where he was regularly beaten by street cleaners from the time he was a tiny puppy on into his adolescence. This horrific and sustained experience means that the following things will never be motivators for him:

- being touched by a stranger
- being approached by a stranger
- being in public, busy places
- going out and about on walks.

Right now, his main motivators are:

- avoiding people, actively running away from them
- sleeping on his owner's bed as it is his safe place
- staying at home and not going out for a walk
- playing at home with his family and the female dog as it is safe.

I only use these to highlight the fact that we do need to stop and think about how and when we use motivators. I have asked this dog's owners to stop walking him for the time being, which seems a crazy thing to ask a responsible dog owner to do. Yet for this dog, a walk is so distressing, and it takes him a long time to recover from it. When he is out in the park he is just running away to get far away from people. It is not fair to subject him to that level of avoidance, fear and distress for the sake of a walk. We can work on that part later.

I'm not giving a specific motivation exercise here, as they will vary so much from dog to dog. But start with working out your dog's motivators and build on these as your relationship develops.

A word of caution

Beware of overusing one particular motivator, such as food or a particular game, as you may inadvertently end up creating an obsession or an unwillingness to accept other options, such as a different toy or treat. Certain breeds can become very obsessive about toys or games, and it is best to avoid this if you can. This can be harder to manage with a rescue dog, whose behaviours may already be difficult to change, but with a puppy you have it within your remit to carve out the motivators you want to use versus those you prefer not to. Do remember that your dog's personality and breed traits will be key in deciphering what your puppy or dog enjoys doing.

RELATIONSHIPS

Everything you do with your dog, including the eye contact and motivator exercises above, builds a better relationship, so I'm not going into huge detail in this section, but I would like you to think of the best relationships you have. Are they characterised by one person always getting their own way? Does one person always have to do what the other person says? Does someone always have to win or beat the other at every game? I'm willing to bet that you have walked away from any relationships that sound like this, as they're no fun at all. And yet so many of us consider a well-behaved dog to be one that does exactly what they're told at all times. I don't personally think this is the right way to build a relationship with your dog.

Good human relationships are built on shared respect, attention and consideration, and the same is true for your relationship with your dog. Time invested in this relationship will be rewarded by a dog who enjoys your company, seeks you out for fun and games, and comes to you for reassurance and love. Who doesn't want that kind of relationship in their life?

As a dog behaviourist, when I meet a new dog it's important to build the relationship between us immediately. I use toys to get the dog to see me as a fun person whom it wants to spend time with, rather than someone who's just bossing it around. I find a great game to play with a dog who is new to you is a tugging game with a toy (the only exceptions being dogs with resource-guarding issues, or an overexcited puppy). Again, you shouldn't always be the one who wins this game. There is some old-fashioned advice that says that you must always win to show the dog who's boss, but in my experience if you always win, the dog will just disengage, and you also run the risk of creating a battle of wills!

I encourage all of my clients to build relationships with their dogs that are based on mutual understanding and respect, and this is the aim of this book! So all of the exercises in the book as a whole will help you build this fun and joyful relationship with your dog, but here are two specific to relationship-building that you can try.

For a toy-motivated dog

Take a pair of old jeans, cut a big strip of denim off (the size of this strip will depend on the size of your dog: for a big dog you could use the entire leg of a pair of jeans, but for a smaller dog just a strip will work). Tie a big, loose knot in the middle of the denim strip and then, sitting on the floor, start moving the denim toy around to get the dog to engage.

At the beginning you will only play for a few minutes, and then put the toy away. Then you'll bring the toy out again, and hopefully your dog will look excited about it. The ideal way to end any game with your dog is with them wanting more, rather than them getting bored.

Once you've got the dog's interest, you can then take the toy behind your back, so that they're actively trying to find it, and then bring it out for them to play with. Ideally this will turn into a tugging game, back and forth.

The next stage will be to start moving around the house and/or garden, and the dog should follow you to continue the fun. You're showing your dog that you're a fun person to be hanging out with.

If a puppy gets too overexcited playing this game and starts biting, just put the toy away. If a dog is more ball-motivated, you can tie a ball into the denim knot to engage them with the game.

For a food-motivated dog

This game uses the same denim strip as above, but this time you put some treats in the loose knot. Give the toy to the dog and allow it to get the treats out – obviously don't make the knot so tight that the dog gives up! Once it's found all the treats, your dog is likely to look at you for more, and then you add more treats into the knot. The key here is getting your dog to see you as the gatekeeper to all the fun!

CHAPTER TEN

What Your Dog Wants You to Know about Sniffing, Snuffling and Snouting

As caring dog owners, we mostly recognise the importance of the dog walk but it seems that many of us have forgotten the actual purpose of it as far as our dogs are concerned. A walk should allow your dog to be stimulated, to fulfil their instincts, using their body and their mind in tandem, not choosing just one or the other to focus on. A dog that is run around the park on the lead without being allowed to stop and sniff and interact with its environment may have been exercised, but it has not had a proper walk by its own standards, and it will not be satisfied with or properly stimulated by the experience.

Think of the ways our dogs were originally bred to work and you'll begin to recognise how much of a whole-body experience life is to a dog:

A Labrador that is working as a gun dog will use its nose

to seek the bird that has fallen, its mouth to retrieve it and its body to run after and bring it back.

A working terrier will use its nose to locate the vermin it's hunting, its mouth to kill them and its body to move on to the next task.

These are just a couple of illustrations to remind you how important all aspects of the dog's body are. Your dog is constantly and naturally yearning to use their mind and their nose; it is just that we often don't notice or recognise these needs.

As owners, even if we recognise that our dog has these needs, we often don't engage with them, so the sniffing and the mental stimulation side of things becomes something your dog goes off and does on its own. We also get caught up in using the dog walk to multitask – the kids need to go to the playground, you need to pick up milk on the way home, etc. These tasks should be extras, not the main event. A dog needs to be walked in a way that allows it to be a dog, and that means sniffing, snuffling and rooting around in its environment (preferably somewhere natural like grass or woods, rather than a pavement or concrete).

I find that sniffing, rooting around and snuffling can be one of the most tiring forms of exercise for a dog. The stimulation it provides can relieve your dog's stress, help it process a situation, learn new things and calm down – it has been proven to lower a dog's heart rate – so let's begin to use it much more.

Some dogs, like Beagles, Foxhounds, Dachshunds and many others, have an insane ability to utilise their noses.

Their ability is incredible and, if you are going to take on a dog with this level of sniffing skill, I'd go as far as to say it is cruel not to allow them to use their nose, as it is their utter joy in life.

There is a video on the internet of a Beagle who smells something cooking inside a worktop oven. He then uses his nose to work out how to solve this conundrum. He pushes a chair against a table, jumps onto the chair and then onto the table, and finally across onto the work surface to the oven. He uses his mouth to pull open the oven door and somehow drags the tray of hot food out. The food lands on the floor and the dog jumps down to eat it. Mission accomplished: that set-up was like a giant, real-life version of a mental stimulation toy and the dog just aced it! Obviously, a dog doing this in your kitchen is not ideal. However, it highlights the need for dogs to problem-solve and use their brains.

There are many, rather less dramatic and destructive ways you can help your dog to use its nose. Some of these are great for dogs who perhaps can't go out for walks due to illness or injury. And while most dogs would rather play with you than alone, some of the sniffing games below can give great entertainment to a dog if you need to keep it entertained while you're busy.

The suitability of each for your own dog will depend on your abilities, your home set-up and what your dog enjoys doing, but here are a few suggestions to get you started. You can use these games for any age of puppy or dog. In fact, I would say that sniffing becomes even more essential for older dogs, as their body is no longer able to walk or run to the level it used to.

- **Snuffle mats**. These interactive toys are the size of a bath mat or smaller and have lots of pieces of long fabric sticking up out of the mat. They make a great, portable place to hide treats, letting your dog use their nose to seek them out. They are easy to make yourself, or you can purchase them via websites like Etsy. I find snuffle mats are a great item for pups and senior dogs alike, to get them using their nose within the home environment. They don't provide long-lasting amusement though; this is a shorter activity.

- **'Find it' games**. There are varying levels of this, but even at the most basic, I think this is a game that all dogs should have in their repertoire. You show the dog an object, like a toy or a treat, and get them to wait while you hide it. Then say 'Find it!' and let the dog seek out the toy or treat. I like to hide things behind cushions or in blankets, where the dog really has to work to find what it's sniffing out. This is where you begin to teach a dog or puppy to utilise their nose on command, and I find this to be one of the best commands your dog can know.

- **Treat-dispensing toys**. These can vary in shape and size and brand. The key to all of them is the dog figuring out how to get the treat out of the toy. You do have to factor in the need to show them how to do this with each toy. Do not expect them to just learn it immediately. If it's too difficult, your dog will just walk away, so bear in mind that it can take a number of weeks to build up to where they can get on and do it all by themselves and to quite a high level of difficulty.

- **Treats under paper cups**. This is a super-simple but

effective way to teach your dog to distinguish between the cup with a treat under it and the ones that don't have one underneath. Kids often delight in playing this game with the dog. Start by simply having two cups: one has a treat under it and one does not. You let your dog sniff and push the cup over to get the treat. You can then start to build on adding in more cups and spreading them further apart to make it a harder game.

- **Sniffing in long grass**. I'm still amazed at the amount of people I see walking their dog along concrete paths when there is a grassy verge to the side. Walk in the grass, people! That is where all the fun stuff for the dog takes place, where the scents rise from, where other creatures tread. Go through the grass rather than around it. Avoid the paths: those are the boring bits for a dog.

- **Visiting new places.** New parks, fields, football pitches and grounds is integral for mixing it up for a dog. The same park becomes boring very quickly. You need to switch it up. When a place you visit becomes too familiar, you will begin to see your dog gradually stop listening, start zoning out and causing mischief, as they know the lie of the land, they know your route. So you do need to be actively factoring in more beneficial walks, not just at the weekend when you have more time. This will be especially important for those dogs who have a high drive, high energy and need outlets.

- **Games.** Depending on your dog's ability and your desire, there are heaps of games you can create for your dog to use their nose. From teaching them how to detect a certain selected essential oil to doing similar with a particular toy that you only use for nose work. The sky is the limit – be led by your and your dog's desires.

Sniffing for a puppy

When you live with a young dog who has energy and you want to get it out but you don't want to just run it for ages, sniffing is your perfect puppy-tiring activity. That might mean going to an area with long grass to snuffle around, or a snuffle mat, as described above, and sitting on your doorstep to entertain your pup with distractions going on in the background.

On walks with a young puppy, I often suggest that rather than just walking down a straight path, which can often be busy and stressful for a young dog, you walk in 'waves'. By that I mean walking back and forth and up and down around the same area. If we walk a puppy in waves, we approach the busy space and then we walk away from it and back into it and away again. This can result in much calmer, easy to manage dogs because we are not constantly expecting perfect behaviour in places that are too overwhelming for them. You can also use sniffing as part of your walking in waves, so that the puppy walks in busy spots and then in sniffy spots, to help them recover and de-stress from the busyness.

By sniffy spots I mean select the walks full of long grass, interesting surfaces to walk on, places where the dog can be free to potter and roam and get immersed in the work of sniffing. Give them an outlet that lowers adrenaline, lowers cortisol and helps them live a more balanced life. You can assess a park or location by its 'sniffage', as in its usage for sniffing. It's certainly not a technical term but an important one for any dog!

If you find that your puppy doesn't want to leave the sniffing areas, it may be that the busier spots are just too much for them. Sniffing can sometimes be used by a dog as a displacement activity, a way to disengage and pretend what is happening doesn't need addressing. Always look out for this, as it may be that you are rushing the puppy too much.

Sniffing for a boisterous, over-the-top dog

Usually when you have a dog full of energy, people start lobbing balls for it, trying to run it into the ground. I always recommend doing the exact opposite: get them using that nose, get them scenting and channelling that energy into something else. Something that will tire them, calm them and replace that focus of chasing a ball.

Chasing a ball relentlessly raises adrenaline. For a dog who is very easy to hype up, the last thing you want is to be encouraging that type of hyper energy, unless you are a police dog handler and you want a dog who is always switched on. Last night I actually stood watching a German Shepherd police dog searching a car that had been pulled over on our street. It was past midnight and this dog was pumped. He was ready to rock, ready to go; he could not have been more willing to work his Shepherd nose off. Which is great if you are the handler of the dog but not so great if you have a pet dog who is fully charged all the time, as it isn't a very relaxing way to live.

Sniffing for a senior dog

As a dog ages, their limbs can lose mobility or they just can't walk as far or for as long as they once could. But they often still want to go for a walk, and to feel a part of their environment. So this is where the smaller, slower, sniffier walks become your best friend. You go at your older dog's pace, you walk like a snail and they spend their time with their nose in the tufts of long grass. Pottering along, enjoying the slower pace of life.

If you have a combination of an older dog and younger dog, or even a puppy, you should look at doing one walk with both older dog and puppy so that the younger one learns to adapt its pace and sees that time can be well spent sniffing along. You should also do another walk for the puppy alone, focusing on what the young dog needs as it still has so much to learn. I'd also make time to take the senior dog[s] out alone, to let them lead it a bit, let them select the pace and when to turn back.

You may start to do shorter walks for an older dog, but more often, for example several ten-minute stints a few times a day. This will maintain mobility and keep your dog interested without overexertion. If you are lucky enough to have a great deal of space or your house backs on to fields, even going and just sitting outside with the dog can encourage them to do a bit more investigative work than if you put them out there alone.

If you don't live somewhere that you have access to that kind of backdrop, you can still drive your dog to interesting sniffing spots. Sometimes even just the car journey, a fifteen-minute sniffing jaunt and a car trip back home are enough for an older dog. I genuinely believe that many of them still want to go out but their bodies just won't allow them, so finding other ways for them to feel included and engaged are still really important.

My mum's rescue dog Barnie was twelve years old when we lost him. In the last two years of his life, when he had really slowed down, we used to drive him to the river in the village where my parents live. We'd just let him have a paddle and drive him back home. When he came to stay with us in London, we just pottered on the street, or sat on the front doorstep watching the world go by. These excursions don't need to be incredible or exciting for an older dog, but they do still usually need a change of scenery and a new sniffing spot.

CHAPTER ELEVEN

What Your Dog Wants You to Know about Chewing

Chewing on items is, I would say, crucial for all dogs. It isn't a nice added bonus or just something to do. It is imperative to their daily life as it:

- helps them process their day, working out any frustration by using their mouth
- can aid calming down by shifting their focus
- provides pain relief for sore gums and teeth
- fulfils a sense of completing a task: there can be a start and a finish
- provides amusement
- can help to encourage independence.

All dogs, no matter their breed, size or age, should be offered daily chewing options that are suitable for them. As much as we might find them fairly revolting, your dog will vastly prefer a chew of animal/fish origin than a rubber bone or similar. These are some of the chewing options that I recommend (below I've suggested some other options for teething puppies, but these can be used for both puppies and adult dogs):

- Himalayan yak chew
- deer antler, split, not whole (make sure it's ethically sourced)
- various edible animal chews that take differing amounts of time to chew, such as dried cow or pig's ears (though these are too fatty for puppies and small dogs). Bull pizzle sticks generally go down a storm: they stink, but dogs love them – just make sure they're not dipped in fat.
- raw bones that are safe for dogs can be excellent, e.g. fresh marrow bones (seek advice from your raw food company)
- dried jerky pieces that are long and thick
- dried sweet potatoes
- dried fish skins.

As a general rule of thumb, I avoid recommending rawhide products, due to the length of time it can take for a dog to digest them, plus many go through a chemical bleaching process, which is less than ideal for when a dog is consuming something.

We do need to be cautious that most of the bull breeds have a tendency to chew on something until it reaches a size that they believe they can just swallow, and they are not always great judges of this! Choking is definitely a hazard. So chewing items do need to be carefully considered and sought out, and it is a good idea to be present when your dog is given a chew.

If your dog shows resource-guarding issues around a chew item, you must seek out behavioural help immediately to make sure you don't exacerbate anything by accidentally reinforcing the guarding behaviour. If in doubt, stop giving chew items until the issue is dealt with.

PUPPY TEETHING

One of the most common issues that my clients get in contact about is struggling with an adorable puppy who one minute is conked out on your lap and the next is propelling themselves off the sofa in order to grab your cardigan or your skin with their needle-sharp teeth. The biting, teething and chewing period can be a tricky time to handle and many people are under the impression that it won't last long. The truth is, no one knows how long teething will last or how long it will take your puppy. There are also factors to consider, such as:

- If your puppy was a single puppy, you may find this period even harder, as they had no litter or siblings to learn from.
- If your puppy was from a huge litter you may also struggle as mum won't have been able to physically discipline and teach them all.
- If you picked up your puppy too early, e.g. five/six/ seven weeks old.
- The breed of dog you have: I find some breeds' teething period can feel way more intense than others, such

as the Border Terrier, the Irish Terrier, the Golden Retriever, the Vizsla and the Staffy, to name but a few. It does of course depend on your dog, though, as they are all different.

The actual process of teething, I find, can start as early as eight weeks old, and it can last for weeks on end. Do not be under the impression that this period will be over in a matter of days! You are in this phase for at least a few months and the severity of it can chop and change, depending on how much their teeth hurt.

Teething is fundamentally where the problems lie: your dog is often in pain and is seeking outlets to meet the need of relieving pain. And a puppy will try any surface, any object, any finger, toe or bodily part that appears to be for the taking. Nothing is out of bounds as they hunt for something to satisfy their needs of relieving pain, getting rid of energy or channelling overstimulation.

Please do not take their biting personally, or believe that your dog has a vendetta against you. I promise this isn't about aggression. Your puppy is simply going to give everything a whirl when it comes to chewing, to see what might meet the need they are trying to satisfy. They are going to jump up, lurch, lunge, attack, chase and grab – it doesn't mean it is acceptable, but you do need to expect this. You need to plan for the teething period rather than just hoping for the best or convincing yourself that your dog won't be like this. Parents with children who bring a puppy home are often shocked at how hard this is to manage. Preparation and a reality check is key here.

You need to then factor in the impact of overtiredness, energy and overstimulation in your puppy, as very often these will produce the same results – a bitey, snappy, difficult to handle dog who may make you want to give up. That feeling is normal, it is usual and if you have kids it can feel even trickier as the kids can often encourage or create problems with the puppy and its mouth of needle teeth.

The absolute key to understanding biting is determining what the reason behind it is, as then you can figure out how to deal with it:

- **Being overhandled**. The dog needs people to leave it alone or put it down.
- **Overtiredness**. The dog needs to rest. This isn't up for debate, it has to happen.
- **Overstimulation**. The dog needs to be removed or the environment needs to change (common in homes with children).
- **Too much energy**. You need to be factoring in how to expend their physical energy and provide outlets for this which are constructive and will not spiral into overstimulation. This often results in people limiting exercise and physical output. Or happens because they have no outside access or room to allow a puppy to roam.
- **Teething**. Their teeth hurt and they are desperately in need of teething items. Bear in mind that you need many, many different options. Dog toy companies like to make it look like their one toy will solve all your dog's needs. It won't. You need a huge selection,

some of which you are in control of and some that they have constant free access to.

- **Anxiety**. I find that anxiety or frustration can show itself through biting on the lead when out and about, or grabbing ankles.

Sometimes we can feel at the end of our tether with the teething period. There will be good days and there will be bad days. It is one of the reasons I recommend a baby gate. If the biting is becoming too much, if you are sick of your clothes being punctured and you have simply had enough, I fully give you permission to sit on one side of the gate, with the puppy on the other side of it, and simply throw tiny treats from your side on to the other. Let the puppy go sniffing and snuffling off after them, let them calm themselves down and forget they were hell-bent on ruining your new trainers. Then re-enter the room with the puppy and see if they are more able to be reasonable. If not, go back on your side of the gate, continue throwing treats like rain from the sky, until they wear themselves out and go splat on the floor! We have to be realistic with teething. Many books tell you to 'ignore the bad and reward the good', but this is just not physically possible all the time. So in that moment, remove yourself, save your sanity, take a deep breath and then start afresh.

Random teething items to utilise for a puppy:

- whole carrots from the fridge: they may eat or just shred them, but either is fine
- chunks of apple (no pips), butternut squash, frozen banana chunks, broccoli stems, cherry tomatoes, etc. Most of this is great on a sensory exploration level, and frozen fruit and veg are cheap too
- old toilet-roll tubes, kitchen-roll tubes and delivery boxes
- plastic bottles with all the labels and lids removed, that teeth can sink into and puncture
- ice cubes: you can freeze bone broth too, to make it more appealing
- scraps of denim or fabric tied into knots
- old magazines: the spine can feel amazing for a puppy to sink their teeth into
- old tea towels
- pieces of hosepipe cut into long chunks
- paper coffee cups you have finished with, rinsed and dried.

Look around your home and really try to use objects that your dog may not be familiar with, as not only is this exercise great for familiarisation and desensitisation to household items, but it can also open the door to lots of different textures, surfaces and sensations. You will of course need to monitor your dog and never leave them alone with an item they are chewing, as they may choke.

It may sound obvious, but avoid giving your dog things

to chew that you don't want them to chew in future. For example, giving them an old shoe might seem like a great idea, but your puppy won't know the difference between this and your brand-new shoe, so try not to build an association for your pup that chewing shoes feels good and is allowed!

CHAPTER TWELVE

What Your Dog Wants You to Know about Body Language

We all know that dogs cannot speak our language, yet somehow they have evolved to navigate their way through our confusing world. For example, you may find that your dog knows when you put on one particular coat that you're going out to work, and when you put on another it's time to go for a walk. It recognises so many tiny cues to anticipate what might come next. Your dog is always watching and learning. Now it is time for us to start taking notice of how our dogs are communicating with us. They're giving us so many visual cues, all the time, and learning to understand these can make the most incredible difference to the life you have with your puppy or dog.

Body language looks different in different breeds, and you will need to learn to recognise when your individual dog is anxious, happy, confident, etc. However, there are some basic principles that are worth knowing, not least so you can spot them in other dogs that your dog may interact with.

Body language in dogs is not 100 per cent straightforward. Ears back can mean happy and relaxed, or frightened, depending on the context. A waggy tail can mean a happy dog or one that may be about to react aggressively. Licking of lips can be something a dog is doing after a delicious meal, or it can be a stress response or a way to let another dog know it's not threatening. Within the space of this book I'm not able to give you a hard and fast list of postures to know, but I can give you some general principles to look out for. What's important is that you are aware of your own dog's body language so you can tell what's going on.

One of the key things to remember is that the way humans and dogs do things is different. It seems obvious but it is worth reminding ourselves. I've often seen images on social media where humans take something that a dog is doing and believe that the dog is replicating the way a human may act. Generally speaking, this is not the case – a human baby being placed next to a sleeping dog does not illustrate they are best friends. We have to be cautious of the way we try to make dogs fit into our own emotional states.

Dogs are highly emotional beings who can learn to be incredibly in tune with us. They can mirror our own emotions, but we must still work to understand what a dog's body, ears, fur, eyes, tail and face are trying to tell us.

A wagging tail does not automatically mean happiness, and a dog rolling over on to its back does not always indicate a desire to be petted on the stomach. These are Disney-esque connotations that we have placed on dogs and this is why sometimes issues arise, as we are watching and understanding incorrect information when the dog responds.

LICKING

I so often see clients touching their puppy or dog, who licks them, and they think this is 'kissing'. But often it is actually a sign that the dog would like to be left alone. It can sometimes be a very kind way of trying to redirect our attentions from one part of their body, usually when we are trying to touch their legs or feet.

A dog that is licking you out of affection will be doing so because it wants to – it will have sought you out to do this. It might be licking your legs when you've just got out of the shower, or it might have come to sit on your lap. However, if you are intruding on your dog's space or restricting or grabbing your dog, or touching it in a way it doesn't like, a lick is how it is trying to ask you to stop. It's about the politest gesture in a dog's body language, so do be aware of it!

SITTING DOWN DURING A WALK

A dog that sits down and doesn't want to move wants you to know that it may be feeling overwhelmed, or that it needs more time. This behaviour is most common with puppies from twelve to sixteen weeks of age, who are just learning about the world around them, but it can also happen with older dogs who may be new to a home or an environment (a dog from the countryside, for example, who finds itself in a city). They may need a moment and it is then down to us to work out whether they simply need a break before carrying on, or whether we need to turn back as they are too overwhelmed to continue. Give them the option, so you can see what they choose to do. I tend to advise against using treats to try to 'lure' them onwards, as if they do just need a break or want to information-gather, we need to let them. A break will enable the dog to move on far more quickly the next time they see, smell or hear that stimulus again, as they will have learned from it and understood it.

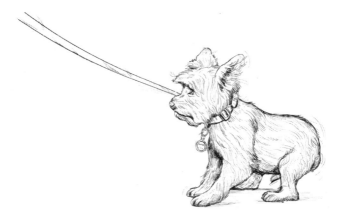

Refusal to move

If this sitting-down behaviour is due to a fear of something or an uncertainty, you need to assess the level of fear. Does the dog look frightened or just uncertain? Is there something specific that your dog is trying to actively get away from (such as a bigger dog, or a new and previously unencountered object like a wheelie bin)? Or is there something that the dog is simply wanting to keep its distance from, such as a noisy vehicle? In either case I would respond by slackening the lead; remove the tension and don't try to pull your dog past whatever is making it anxious. Instead, let them show you what they need: they might want to get past it, or scurry back to you, to simply observe, or to sit between your feet for protection. Let them tell you, instead of constantly rushing from A to B. Dogs don't know your destination!

If the sitting behaviour is down to a puppy needing to sit, learn, watch, observe and listen, again I would allow them to do so. Information-gathering for puppies, and some older dogs, is so underrated. Rather than have it set in your head that you will take a thirty-minute walk to the coffee shop and then on to the park, just go at your pup's pace and see how far you get. Go with the flow and allow your pup to engage with the world in its own time. You may think you don't have time for this, but if you don't allow them to learn and fathom out whether new objects and experiences are good, bad or ugly, it may create more fear-related behaviours later on in life.

I promise you this phase won't last for ever, but it is a key part of allowing a puppy or a dog to gain understanding and awareness of their new environment.

It is worth bearing in mind, particularly with older dogs, that they may refuse to walk because they are in pain. This may be due to an injury, illness or joint pain due to arthritis. If this refusal to walk persists, you may want to take a trip to the vet to ensure there is no medical reason the dog is sitting down on walks.

Some dogs will also genuinely get bored of certain walks, if you are doing the same route, park or journey every single day. I know of a little Dachshund who did this during lockdown. He started sitting stubbornly on the doorstep as he just didn't fancy the same place each day, so he would rather not go!

CLAWING AT YOUR LEGS

As a signal from a dog to its owner, I think the scrabbling at your legs gets overlooked a great deal, and people often push the dog away and tell it to stop. Please don't ignore it. If your dog keeps scrabbling at your legs, scrabbling for attention, it is trying to tell you something. Look at the environment you are in. Is it too much for the dog? Are too many people trying to pet it? Are there too many other dogs around or is there too much dog-on-dog interaction?

I find that this behaviour is very common from the long-limbed dogs such as Hungarian Vizslas, German Short-haired Pointers and Whippets, but you can find this with many other breeds too.

*Clawing or scratching at your legs is your dog
trying to tell you something*

If your dog claws at your legs in a busy situation, simply try walking off with your dog, exiting the group of people standing chatting in the park or walking away from the gang of playing dogs. See if the behaviour of scrabbling at your legs ceases. If so, you have your answer: the dog wanted to get out of an overwhelming situation. You may find that the dog then stops scrabbling and turns to sniffing the ground, and the further you go they can then raise their head and refocus on you as they feel more comfortable. These are tiny signals but super-important ones to take note of, as paying attention and taking action can prevent your dog becoming aggressive or reactive to other dogs in the future.

HIDING BEHIND YOUR LEGS

Both puppies and dogs will do this in the park, on the street or at a café when they are anxious, and this behaviour should always be validated. By which I mean, if your dog wants to hide away it is looking for help and protection from you: respect that and allow it. Never ever pull your dog out from behind your legs. If you are sitting down, don't lift your legs up, as you simply expose your dog and make its seeking of help fruitless. I would always encourage and reward a dog who chooses to exit a situation. It is a good thing when your dog chooses a flight instinct instead of opting for the fight instinct. Do bear in mind that, if you keep removing the flight option from them, they may only be left with an alternative that you like even less: to use aggression.

Hiding is a request to be left alone

If someone approaches and your dog does not want to say hello, does not want to approach, does not want contact and most definitely does not want to play, then please do not make them do any of those things. Their fear or worry must be respected.

If your dog is hiding, this is not the time to start using treats to try and lure your dog into wanting contact. By that I mean don't give the child your dog is avoiding a treat in an attempt to create a connection. This action will simply pair fear with food in your dog's mind, and I'm really not a big fan of that kind of linking. I'd rather your dog was just allowed to acclimatise at their own rate, or perhaps they will always be the kind of dog who never seeks out a stranger's contact, and that is fine too. I would also actively remove a dog from a situation if it shows it doesn't want to interact or be part of something.

PANTING AND DROOLING

We often attribute panting to a dog being warm. The reality is that it is much more likely to be your dog showing either a stress reaction or a relief reaction, especially if the weather is not hot.

Panting can help a dog regulate itself, so when it feels stressed you may notice it quite soon begins to pant. Depending on the situation, you can find that an anxious dog's breath starts to smell differently from usual – for example, stress panting on a car journey. This kind of stress panting may trigger the glands in their throat, which can sometimes then make their breath smell.

Do pay attention to sustained panting from your dog. If it is panting a lot in a particular situation, it may be a sign that your dog is feeling anxious and overwhelmed. It may be worth removing the dog from that situation to see if it is more relaxed elsewhere.

Dogs will also pant out of happiness to see you – for example, when you return from work or after a couple of hours' absence – but that kind of panting will stop very quickly, and isn't sustained.

Continual, excessive panting out of nowhere can also indicate pain in a dog, or an inability to get comfortable or find relief.

A DOG IN PAIN

There is little that feels worse for a caring dog owner than discovering your dog has been in pain without you noticing. The guilt can be awful, but the truth is that dogs often try to mask their pain, so it's good to know some signs you can look out for that your dog is struggling, is in pain and could be suffering:

- an inability to get comfortable or stay in one position for very long
- not sleeping deeply
- or sleeping deeply but doing nothing else, as if shutting out the world
- panting, for what appears to be no reason
- they spin around abruptly if you touch them
- if you try to touch a part of their body, they may try

to redirect your touch somewhere else, e.g. from their back to their head
- excessive licking of a body part
- they growl or bite when you touch an area on their body.

Some signs are of course more obvious, such as limping, not weight-bearing on a leg, constantly scratching an ear, discharge from an area, etc. All of these should be brought to your vet's attention.

Do bear in mind, though, that not all dogs in pain will show it during an examination, e.g. a dog who was born with an issue may have learned to live with the pain as it is all that they know, but it doesn't mean that the pain isn't there. We do have to be careful not to dismiss pain in dogs just because we can't see it. My dog Pip is very stoic. His previous home shut down his attempts to show emotion, so he holds it in, but it doesn't mean that he doesn't still feel it. If you truly feel that there is a pain-related issue but you can't detect the source, you can talk to your vet about a pain trial, to see if the removal of the pain (using pain relief medication) changes their behaviour. I am about to embark on this with Pip for a month, as I suspect his back end is starting to cause aggravation but he isn't showing what some may say are the classic signs.

'THEY'RE JUST PLAYING!' OR BODY LANGUAGE WITH OTHER DOGS

It is essential to understand your dog's body language with

other dogs in order to avoid issues of aggression, fear and intimidation. You will often hear dog owners in the park suggest that dogs will 'sort things out themselves' or that they are 'just playing', but dogs need to learn their manners around other dogs in order to live harmoniously.

In my opinion a well-mannered dog is one who does not bolt into other dogs' faces and jump on them. It will stick pretty close to its owner on walks, it will listen to you, it will look for you. It will respond to its name and it will not cause havoc around other people or other dogs or animals. It comes back when it is called.

There is no perfect dog, but as owners we can aim for reliability and predictability. We can work on teaching these manners, knowing that some things take longer than others. And when we know our dog isn't capable of being well mannered around other dogs or people, we as an owner can be responsible by not putting the dog in a situation it can't cope with. Or we can simply pop it on a lead so that its unwanted behaviours don't distress other people or their pets.

We often tolerate interactions or behaviours between dogs because other owners have told us 'It's fine, it's just play' or 'I wouldn't worry, you want her to be taught a lesson' and similar phrases. I actively say, if it feels too much, get your dog or puppy out of a situation. In terms of what I define as 'too much', this could be:

- no breaks in the play
- play isn't reciprocal or being taken in turns
- one dog looks like it is being pummelled by another/ others

- the interaction looks too intense
- one of the dogs is trying to exit or run away
- one dog is being chased constantly
- there is a lot of barking going on
- nipping starts happening
- your puppy or dog loses the ability to listen or look for you, and it may even bolt off
- a puppy is constantly trying to remove themselves, walking off, head turning away, sniffing the ground – it does not want to engage.

These are just a few examples to look out for. Also bear in mind that just because a breed will naturally play that way does not make it fine. For example, a Whippet will naturally chase, but when the chase gets too stimulating they may begin to nip at the backs of necks or tails of other dogs. This isn't fine, and needs to be stopped. It can only start to escalate and become a default behaviour, which we definitely do not want to encourage.

When it comes to a puppy being taught a lesson by another dog, I definitely do not want this to be done via brute force, aggression or fear, as this can and will imprint on them. It can backfire in the long run by contributing to creating a 'reactive dog'.

Owners of big boisterous dogs, especially young ones, often take the opposite view, which is that it's *their* dog who needs to be taught a lesson by other dogs. Rather than prevent their dog from harassing another dog, they will wait for the harassed dog to growl, snarl or even try to bite. If you've ever wondered why small dogs have a reputation for being aggressive, it's because many of them have learned they have to be proactive in getting bigger, bouncy dogs to leave them alone. It is not just aggression that we need to watch out for, but a situation that a dog feels it cannot escape from. Always look to manage your own dog, and the situation you are in, instead of expecting another dog to do that for you.

If your dog needs to learn a lesson, it is you who must do the teaching, kindly showing them how you want them to react. Taking the time and putting the effort in to begin to help your dog will pay dividends in the future.

It isn't another dog's job to discipline your puppy, and it isn't their role to get so annoyed with your dog that they feel they have to reprimand them. It is up to you as the owner to take control, to keep your dog with you, to not allow them to bolt away from you and towards other dogs. And if you cannot do this, which is common with a puppy who is learning, then you must take steps to teach them using a five-metre long line (not an extendable lead) and work with a behaviourist to achieve the long-term goals you have for your dog.

It isn't safe for your dog to run into another dog. If that dog were to tell your dog off so badly that they were to be physically injured and mentally scarred, it would be your fault. I know that can sound harsh, but we have to be respectful of each other, we have to give dogs and owners space, we have to recognise that it is not a puppy's right to run into every dog it sets eyes on. In the eyes of the law, if your dog is deemed 'out of control', this is also an offence and this can be applied to any breed of dog. If you cannot 'control' your dog, a member of the public would be within their legal rights to report you, and your dog could be seized, whether it is a Chihuahua or an Irish Wolfhound.

I understand that it can feel uncomfortable to have to turn down your dog playing with a friend's dog or someone's dog in the park. Saying no and walking away can feel like you are being rude or judgemental. But if you don't think it's the right dog for your dog to be playing with, it is far better to be thought rude than it is to end up with a dog who is aggressive, reactive and difficult around other dogs due to its puppyhood exposures.

A woman with a Cavalier King Charles Spaniel told me about a seven-month-old puppy in her building. The puppy's owner wanted to initiate playtime between her pup and the spaniel, but it was clear that the spaniel really didn't enjoy the interactions. It just kept trying to get away from the bouncy puppy, but the spaniel's owner felt awkward saying no to the puppy's owner because they were neighbours. If I kept being punched in the face every time I saw a certain friend, I certainly wouldn't be speed-dialling them up for a social meet-up! These kinds of aversive situations and associations can cause long-term detrimental feelings around other dogs. So you are far better to cut your losses, be perceived as slightly rude, and end up with a joyful dog to share your life with.

If your puppy is living with older dogs, remember it is not their responsibility to reprimand the puppy. Do not fall into the trap of believing that the older dogs should do all the work on your behalf.

Many older dogs find puppies a bit too much. For puppies, play is a dress rehearsal for life. They are learning new skills, learning to adapt, figuring out what they can and can't do, and what differs from the things they learned with their litter. They will be starting to explore where the boundaries lie, when to stop, when to start up again and they can learn this extremely well from other dogs, as long as those dogs are patient and well behaved.

But you do also have to watch out that they don't pick up bad habits. A puppy who is regularly allowed, for example, to pull on another dog's harness or collar in play may get an unpleasant surprise when it tries the same behaviour with a dog who won't tolerate this. Or, if you have a French Bulldog puppy who only ever plays with other Frenchies, she may expect that all dogs play in the same way as her breed, which is to upturn, push over, be boisterous and rough in their play. But many breeds and dogs dislike that way of playing, which could lead to the French Bulldog getting itself into a great deal of trouble when she's older.

Consider the behaviour you hope for from your adult dog, and begin that work from the very beginning of your relationship. Your dog won't become a mature and confident pup without you putting the work in.

It is equally important to restrict your dog's focus on other dogs during walks. Their focus should be on you (see pages 136–147 for eye-contact exercises), so you must work hard to be the life and soul of the walk with your dog. Yes, this is time-consuming and hard work, but it definitely pays off in the long run.

A client once said to me, during an outside session, 'When can I stop putting this much effort in?' and the answer is never! We should always be going out with treats and toys in our bags, ready to play, to reward and have some fun.

HOW SHOULD MY DOG INTERACT WHEN MEETING OTHER DOGS?

When two dogs are sussing each other out for the first time, I always like to see what I call the C-shaped curve of investigation (see picture).

The canine version of a polite head-nod greeting

This is the ideal shape that two dogs should assume when they encounter each other. The C-shaped curve should feel fluid, soft and not scary to either dog. It is merely a way of sniffing each other's rear ends, gaining information about each other, deciding whether to carry on interacting, to play, to walk away or engage. If your dog does not like other dogs coming up to them from behind, which can be common due to an early puppy experience or due to impacted anal glands, you will need to be very ready to respond and to reward your dog for removing themselves from the sniffing dog. You may also want to consider teaching them an instant 'sit', so that the dogs cannot reach the bottom area. I'd only recommend this if your dog has established issues with the anal glands or some kind of traumatic experience linked to that area of their body.

The C-shaped interaction is essentially the canine version of a polite head nod between two dogs. Ideally it should be a brief curve by each dog, a sniff and a walk on. It is important that we teach our dogs to walk past another dog without always needing to interact. But if they are going to interact then this is a nice way of doing it. Do try to reward the walking-on part with you, when your dog exits the curve of sniffing!

Many puppies will want to approach a dog via the nose first, but as they get older this doesn't happen so much, as they learn to use the C-shaped curve to investigate each other.

DOG-TO-DOG POSTURES TO NOTE

Tense posture

Tense posturing in a dog can appear intimidating to other dogs. By 'tense posturing', I mean a dog that looks intensely alert; their body looks hard; their tail is up, and may be wagging but not in a relaxed, friendly manner. This posture, even if unintended, may be perceived as a sign of tension or confrontation, and can cause issues with other dogs.

Tense body language can include intense staring, raised hackles and
tail, a rigid posture, lack of response to commands, and growling

There are some breeds that naturally have a more tense posture, such as many of the bull breeds (Staffordshire Bull Terrier, Pit Bull, English Bulldog, Bull Terrier, French Bulldog). They will adopt a stance of being very still, very tense and very alert, and this can make some dogs feel uncomfortable. Other dogs may try to give a tense-postured dog a wide berth when walking past. A dog that is concerned may start sniffing the ground as they go past, as they may just want to limit their interactions with these kinds of assertive postures.

That means, as a dog owner, if you have a dog who postures like this, you need to be really 'on it' to avoid unnecessary altercations. I recently encountered a guy walking his dog, a huge, crossbreed bitch who was very intense. She stared at other dogs, her posturing was hard, and she was also physically very large. Her owner was on his phone, far from his dog, who was off lead, running up to and into every dog, and with this very full-on posturing that could easily have led to a fight. In human terms it would be the equivalent to an unknown person running at you and immediately posturing to begin a fight. Although the dog wasn't biting or attacking, it was causing a lot of anxiety for other dogs and owners. This situation can be easily avoided if a dog with this kind of posturing and behaviour is under control, on a lead or has decent recall, but none of the above were true in this case.

Interaction with flatter-faced breeds

Dogs with flat faces, such as Pugs, Boxers and French Bulldogs, can also unnerve other breeds, as sometimes their breathing, especially if more laboured, can sound like growling or may be offensive to another dog. They also cannot physically exhibit the same amount of facial expression as some other breeds, due to their facial muscles and capabilities. It is helpful to remember that flatter-faced breeds need to get their full face up against something, whether it be a surface, a person or a dog, in order to intake scent as, unlike other dogs, they do not have a long muzzle to suck scent into. So their systems of interacting can be more intense for some other dogs to tolerate. If you see other dogs trying to get away from your flat-faced dog, respect this, teach your dog to stay close to you and make sure your dog doesn't just run up to and into every dog.

The roll over on the back

This posture is extremely common with puppies when encountering other dogs, usually signalling that the puppy is worried, and wanting to ensure it is not seen as a threat by another dog. Other dogs will also do this into adolescence, but it may then progress into snippy, nippy, snarly behaviour, if their attempt to disengage isn't respected. If you are noticing that your puppy or dog is doing this frequently, you should seek to adapt the way the interactions with other dogs are taking place – firstly stop allowing dogs to run up to and into your dog. Walk with dogs who are respectful and will leave your puppy alone; do not keep putting your dog into the situation of feeling vulnerable and intimidated. This posture is one of fear and anxiety. Do not be told otherwise, or mistake it for what some label as 'submission'.

This pup is fearful of the others,
and indimidated rather than submissive

If your dog is rolling on to its back a great deal, you need to look at the circumstances surrounding this behaviour. So if, for example, it is to do with the approach of other dogs, you need to seek out a behaviourist to assist you with finding the right way to help your dog gain confidence (and see page 205 for tips on building confidence). You often hear people explain the rolling over by saying that their dog is such a flirt, just wants their belly rubbed all the time. In fact it isn't either of these at all. While it can feel harmless, you really don't want your dog lacking so much in confidence that they feel too worried or anxious to do anything other than roll over.

Making sure your dog isn't being bullied or constantly being placed in situations with people or dogs who create this behaviour in your dog is important too. Examining the dogs your dog goes out with when in daycare or with a walker is imperative, as constant exposure to dogs who are intimidating them may result in your dog starting to get bitey with those dogs. So we want to prevent that happening.

Tail wagging

This is the one piece of dog body language that everyone thinks they know – a wagging tail means that a dog is happy. Right? Not exactly. A dog will wag its tail for other reasons than happiness as well. We must not forget that part of the purpose of a dog's tail wag is to waft around the scent from their anal glands.

A dog can still wag its tail if it gets into a scrap or a fight: this wag will feel and look rather different from a relaxed and happy one, but to the untrained eye could be mistaken for 'wagging'. So you need to be paying attention to the position of the tail, the speed it moves, how high it's held, and whether it is up or down.

Get to know the tail wags of your own dog as there is no one-size-fits-all description here; this is down to your breed or crossbreed. For example, some of the sight-hounds will tuck their tails under when worried, whereas a Labrador's tail may still keep moving. You can also find that some breeds, such as the Pug, who has a curly tail, will use their tail differently as it doesn't physically wag. It may move a bit but it moves differently from, say, a Boston Terrier that has no tail at all. You should be starting to see the intricacies within the apparently simple action of a dog wagging its tail! Spending time on watching your dog pays dividends. If you are out walking your dog, have your partner or a friend take videos or slo-mo videos of your dog interacting and watch them back. This can be enormously helpful to uncover the teeny-tiny details you are missing.

UNDERSTANDING AGGRESSION IN DOGS

So much aggression in dogs can arise from fear, and a frightened dog will start to indicate its discomfort or anxiety by using very subtle physical signals. It is important to have an awareness of these signals, as a dog will slowly begin to escalate its signals of aggression if the subtle, calmer ones do not work.

Do bear in mind that puppy-farmed, badly bred, poorly

socialised, abused or neglected dogs may have never been taught how to respond properly to their fear by an attentive mother. They may have had all of their fear signals ignored by those who were breeding them, or they may have been through trauma that affects the processes a dog will take to remedy a situation. So always exercise more caution with dogs from a troubled background.

Something that all owners should be aware of is what I like to call the 'traffic lights of aggression'. This is also sometimes called 'the ladder of aggression', but I have found that using the colour and light scheme of traffic lights not only helps hammer the point home visually but also makes it easier for children to understand.

If we are standing looking at a set of traffic lights, we understand that the green light means to be calm, relaxed and on your way. The amber means to start to get ready to take action of some kind. And the red light means you do not even attempt any kind of movement – it is the equivalent to someone using capital letters in an email or being shouted at. We are taught about traffic lights very early on: they are visual, they do not need words and they are very easy for anyone to grasp, no matter where you are from, what language you speak or your background – which, for me, is why I think we should start using them to understand a dog's body language.

While all dogs are different, I base the traffic-light system on the 'usual' behaviour of a dog that has no hearing or sight issues, and has been bred well and socialised properly.

MY TRAFFIC-LIGHT SYSTEM
FOR DOGS

Green

This is where the dog starts to use very calm, non-confrontational behaviours to get away from a situation it does not like. These will vary a little but some common ones may be:

- getting up and walking away
- ears going backwards
- removing themselves from a situation, person or place
- blinking in quick succession
- turning their head away gently
- licking their lips
- yawning
- body shakes, as if shaking off water from the fur
- rolling on to their back out of intimidation
- licking of your hands, especially if you are trying to touch them (see page 175 on licking)
- tail tucked underneath their back legs
- going behind someone's legs, under a table
- jumping up, scrabbling at their owner's legs
- tensing their mouth
- puffing their mouth – opening and closing.

The best-case scenario for both owner and dog is that these green-light signs are recognised and acted upon.

The dog is removed from the situation, person or other dog, and it no longer feels fearful. If the dog's green-light signals are repeatedly ignored and actually don't work to create distance, remove stimulus, remove the thing they are fearful or worried about, then the dog has no choice except to move into the amber-light actions. In a well-bred litter of puppies, a puppy who doesn't like something, or doesn't want to play, will simply get up and stumble or tumble away, creating distance. They learn this from a very young age, and it is imperative that we as humans continue to respond to it.

Amber

Amber signs are the ones that we as humans often consider to be rude or unnecessary, such as snapping or growling at people or other dogs. I frequently meet dogs that have been told off for using this level of action because we as owners don't like it very much. It can be embarrassing for dog owners when their dog air snaps but, like it or not, these behaviours are more likely to get noticed than the green-light ones that will have been ignored.

- lip curling
- tense body posture
- slow head turns
- quiet, low-level growling
- freezing behaviour
- eyes will stare and fixate
- air snapping, i.e. biting into the air

- slow tick-tock tail
- beak punching, where their muzzle tries to punch at something
- barking
- lunging
- nipping – not piercing the skin but teeth make contact
- muzzle punching – where nose goes in and can bruise skin.

The amber signals are starting to head into warning territory. There is still room for manoeuvre, but if these signs and actions get blocked, ignored or missed over and over again, it really leaves the dog only one place to go.

Red

A red traffic light spells danger. The same is true in this situation for a dog. The dog has tried its hardest to be calm, collected, non-confrontational, and to take the removal option, but it hasn't worked. I always liken this situation to giving someone a toolbox full of useful, handy, helpful tools and then over time we remove each tool from the box, until all that person is left with is a hammer. A hammer is good for knocking down walls but not ideal for lots of other jobs.

The actions used when a dog feels like it only has red-light tactics left will not be ones that we as humans are comfortable with. We will recognise these actions as aggression and we will want to put a stop to them immediately. The

behavioural issue now is that the dog has learned the green
and amber options don't work, and it may go straight to red
in future.

- lunging with intention to bite
- full teeth baring
- growling with intention of keeping something away
- bullying, stalking behaviour to keep on top of something, e.g. another dog
- freezing and growling at the same time
- launching to bite and bite properly
- savaging with the mouth.

As you can imagine, the red zone can feel very scary and
can create a great deal of damage for humans and other
dogs. It can also result in a dog being put to sleep immediately for fear over their capabilities.

I raise this traffic-light system not to scare you, but to
empower you on your journey with your puppy or dog.
If your dog spends their whole life using the green-light
actions, and having you respond to them, they won't need
to move up to amber and eventually red.

When I used to work with youth offenders and rescue
dogs, I used to discuss the traffic-light system with them,
using the analogy of a person standing on a bus. Imagine
being on a bus when a person gets on and stands so close
to you that their face is in yours. It doesn't feel nice or
comfortable and you would like it to stop.

In this situation, your actions may look something like
this:

Green

- saying 'Excuse me, please could you move?'
- turning your face away
- holding your breath
- shifting to the side, but then they follow you
- stepping away, but they follow you.

Amber

- starting to gently push the person away
- beginning to sound irate when asking them to move away
- threatening other actions
- you may start to sweat and your adrenaline kicks in
- talking through gritted teeth
- you may start to raise your voice.

Red

- shoving and pushing the person away with much more intent
- you may begin to shout
- some people would begin to hit and use physical force
- likely to swear and be very confrontational.

I feel that deciphering this process can make us much more able to empathise and help our dogs out of difficult and potentially dangerous situations. Our long-term goal is not to 'cure' aggression but to learn how to prevent a risky situation from developing in the first place. Understanding these signs early enough could also help thousands of dogs from being put into rehoming centres and put to sleep.

CHAPTER THIRTEEN

What Your Dog Wants You to
Know about Confidence

To me, a confident dog is one who is calm, has no need to use aggression with either other dogs or humans, and does not push themselves on other dogs or people. A confident dog can settle and relax into a situation and not have a constant fear of missing out on what is happening elsewhere.

On the other side of the coin, a lack of confidence can manifest in dogs in many ways, from being too scared to be left alone, to being anxious, fearful and aggressive around others. Many call this behaviour 'dominance' but I don't believe in this term for pet dogs. I've never met a dog yet whose sole intent and purpose was to dominate its owner, take over its owner's life and bathe in the glory of that success. What I do see time and time again are dogs who don't have boundaries. They feel worried, they feel fearful and they lack confidence.

One thing I can say for absolute certain is that building confidence in your dog will not come from being pushed into facing its fears. Pushing your dog to do something it is afraid of will make it more frightened, not less, and the fear is likely to get worse.

Recently I worked with a couple whose puppy was terrified of other dogs, so friends had advised it should go to daycare, to 'socialise' and learn. It didn't help, as the dog was too scared to learn anything except that its fears about other dogs were justified: that other dogs are scary, bad things happen and they won't leave me alone. What that puppy needed was quiet, calm, well-managed interactions with the right kinds of dogs who could help the puppy build its confidence, not tear it down and make it irreparable as an adult.

Please don't force your dog to do things it doesn't want to do in order to 'toughen up'. Dogs, like humans, respond best to empathy, understanding and love. And that's a more fun process for both of you.

FOOD AND CONFIDENCE

As mentioned earlier, some people will try to use food to instil confidence in their dog. For example, if the dog is terrified of the postman, they might suggest that the postman gives the dog a treat to create a positive association. Put simply, don't do it. The last thing you want to teach a fearful dog is to go in, swipe food from a hand and then dart away. The only thing that dog will learn is to go into the thing they are fearful of, to approach it head-on and then dive off. Whereas if we just didn't make these kinds of pairings, we would give dogs far more space to watch and learn from the situation, with nothing bad being re-inforced.

Food has some brilliant uses for working with dogs, but it isn't as simple as giving a random stranger some dried liver to pass to the dog and all its nervous fear will dissipate and diminish for ever. If it were that simple, no dog would have an issue with strangers. We can look at using food to desensitise a dog, but this is a much more drawn-out process than someone simply handing your dog food.

I would only use food with fearful dogs if I was doing very precise work around rewarding different body-language cues or ways of changing their reaction, e.g. rewarding a dog for walking away from a person.

HOW TO BUILD CONFIDENCE IN A DOG

I honestly believe that a well-bred, properly socialised dog should not have huge areas of concern when it comes to confidence. There may of course be areas that need some work with a puppy, but I wouldn't expect the larger issues like I often see in rescue dogs and puppies that have been bred poorly.

During the pandemic I've seen many more dogs than ever before with confidence issues, manifesting as debilitating fear around new people, new situations and environments. For me, this is not solely about socialising a puppy. It has more to do with the appalling nature of how these dogs have been bred. Not being able to go to a pub is not the founding reason for your dog being scared! Actually,

I found the pandemic was an ideal time to socalise a puppy as there were fewer distractions about, so the acclimatisation could be more gradual and less intense. Which is actually ideal: people were still on the streets, parks were still open and cars were still on the road. If your pandemic puppy has struggled, I'm afraid it is likely to have more to do with its breeding than lockdown.

I met a twenty-four-week-old Border Collie puppy recently. Her owners had bought her from a woman who lived alone in remote Wales, where she had no visitors at all when the puppies were young. The owners then picked up the puppy and brought it home to London. The vet messed up their vaccinations and the puppy didn't start going out of the house until it was sixteen weeks old. By the time I was called in, the dog had severe fear aggression and this wasn't down to the pandemic; this was down to the fact that the dog, from the day it was born, had never met any other people or dogs or encountered any objects like vehicles. The pandemic didn't cause this situation; that dog was simply not suitable to come and live with a busy family in West London.

Confidence-building play with you

Playing is a key area to help a dog build confidence. It is a very slow burn, though, and should be led by your dog. Take a look at your dog's current level of play, and work from where they are. If you are beginning to introduce a ball, for example, don't automatically grab the ball and start throwing it, just put the ball down and let your dog interact with it a bit. Roll it around on the floor for a while. Let them guide you. We don't want to overexert our role and actually hinder our dog's ability to play or interact.

Try not to be overbearing in your play or games. Worry less about the 'rules' and be more concerned with just inciting some joy and interaction with you. Really pay attention to your dog's motivators for this.

Confidence-building play with other dogs

Playing with other dogs can build confidence, too. Find a confident dog whom yours bonds well with; this can unlock that ability to let themselves go in play. I find that rescue dogs who are fearful of people can learn to change their perception of people by spending time with a reliable, people-loving dog who can show them that humans can be trusted.

Confidence-building play with interactive toys

Playing with an interactive toy can be incredibly useful to allow a dog to swell with pride at its own achievements. This could be a treat-dispensing toy or it could be showing a dog how to fetch; whatever floats your dog's boat is what you must use. Make a game challenging enough to be interesting, but not so challenging that your dog loses confidence rather than gaining it.

For example, my rescue dog Pip was quite shut off from lots of things when he arrived. I started dropping treats into an empty cardboard box for him to pull out, but this was too much for him, and he had absolutely no idea what I was doing. So I used this method as my marker of where we were at with building his confidence around new objects. For around a year, in small increments over many, many days, I broke down the scariness of the box for Pip. We started with putting a treat on top of a flat piece of cardboard – he was happy to take this off and eat it. We built up the game until Pip was happy to take treats from a shallow box and have slowly progressed from there. We are now at the point where I can take a large box, fill it with scrunched-up paper and Pip is now confident enough to shove his entire head in, snuffle around and even drag the whole box into his bed. This would never have happened in the early days, and it's been a slow process, but so worthwhile. It's also lovely to see the joy he takes from this game.

Give plenty of chewing time

As I mentioned earlier, chewing allows a dog to process situations and feelings. It allows them time to reflect and to let out any frustration. So if your dog is lacking in confidence it's a great idea to give it plenty of time to chew. Find items that vary in length of time for them to chew so that you can allocate an item depending on how frustrated, anxious or pent-up they are. See page 166 for suggested chewing items.

Don't rush!

Don't rush confidence-building. That advice is relevant for all parts of life (for dogs and humans!), but pushing through and skipping steps won't help a dog adjust any quicker to an uncertain situation. Like I mentioned about the sitting on the street, letting them live within a situation and giving them the time to work through it is super important.

Don't interrupt sleep

Sleep is an important escape for an under-confident dog and it can be a way of processing all that has taken place. Don't interfere with your dog's off switch because of your own timetable.

More confidence-building techniques

- Provide all the snuffly, sniffly opportunities you can, especially if walks invoke fear around people and dogs. Try to change their initial expectations and show them that walks now mean the joy of sniffing. Look at where you walk and adjust to quieter areas.
- Adjust your expectations. We expect all dogs to be the waggling Labrador who wants everyone to pet them and that just isn't true. Different is fine; you just learn to change the situations you put your dog into.
- Identify the situations, places, dogs and people that

your dog thrives with and do more with them. Pip has a dog he loves, Bowie, and Nellie and Gus whom he was fostered with. Seeing them definitely gives him some confidence.

- Identify the situations, places, dogs and people that your dog dislikes, or that invoke fear, and keep your distance and do far less with them.
- Make life a bit predictable. You don't need to be on a military regime, but a certain degree of knowledge of what happens next can provide comfort for many fearful dogs. What we then have to watch out for is that this doesn't spill into obsessions, e.g. around food feeding times, the ball, etc.

CONFIDENCE-BUILDING TASKS

You must bear in mind with these that it will depend on your dog and the reason for their individual lack of confidence. Which is why I've tried to make these suitable for all dogs without being too specific:

1. Shredding. Providing objects that they can shred and rip apart is incredibly satisfying – carrots, huge cabbage leaves, hunks of cucumber, a rolling apple chunk (no pips).
2. Destroying. Purposefully giving them items to 'destroy' is, I find, cathartic and fulfilling for many dogs. Let them rip the arm off a toy, pull the squeaker out, rip off the tennis-ball trim. There is a joy in the completion of the task for them.

3. Identify areas of fear, e.g. sound sensitivity, and make sure your games aren't compounding that fear; a ball hitting a fence, trying to teach 'fetch' with a toy that whistles and so on.

4. Treat-dispensing toys. Make them incredibly easy to begin with, so that they get really involved and invested in the toy, and very slowly, in tiny steps, make it harder over the coming weeks. Be there to praise them as they succeed.

CHAPTER FOURTEEN

What Your Dog Wants You to Know about Play

This may be the longest chapter in the book, and that is because play is so much more important for our dogs than many of us imagine. I get asked all the time about food, separation anxiety, toilet-training and yet I have never once had anyone ask me about how to play with their dog. If you take one thing away from this book, let it be that playing is essential for a happy dog and a happy owner, and that it has a real role in everyday life.

Sometimes my clients ask me when do I stop the treats, the play and the training with my dog? The short answer is never! A happy, confident, fulfilled dog is one who is engaged with regularly, gently challenged at times, and rewarded. You absolutely can teach an old dog new tricks and doing so will keep it bonded with you even more strongly.

I like to think of treats, play and training as the salary we pay to our dogs for being a dog. Most people work for payment, and dogs need payment too in the form of incentives and rewards! You will be able to mix and match and vary the rewarding items you use and when you use them. You may not need to reward as frequently once your dog leaves puppyhood, depending on your dog and its behaviour. But even if you do need to, don't worry about it. I would much rather you continued rewarding until the day your dog dies than withdrawing it all just because you think you should.

Over the years, our lives change, the ways we live alters and the same is true of our dogs. We may move, we may have family changes, there may be happiness, sadness and much more in-between. Our beloved dogs will be by our side throughout it all, so it isn't unusual that our dogs may need some additional help or guidance along the journey too. When you bring a new baby home, we have to factor in how to make that child a positive addition for the dog, and reinforcements like games and toys can be a brilliant way to link them to the new human. For example, when the baby's feeding you might throw treats for your dog, or play fetch, so that the dog's not ignored all the time in favour of the baby. Each dog differs, but knowing what your dog sees as rewarding is a key component.

The key is using rewards that suit what you are trying to either teach or reinforce with your dog. For example, if you are trying to stop a dog jumping up to grab a ball, to get you to play, I wouldn't start with using the ball as the reward for not jumping up. We need to start with something less interesting to begin with and work up.

I have dog clients whom I have known since they were eight weeks old and I continue to know, learn about and work with them throughout their entire lives. The reinforcers we used when they were tiny puppies will be different from the ones I use when I work with them at three years old and eight years old. I think it is important to be adapting and changing what we use according to the dog's energy levels, their likes and dislikes. Like us, these things change as we age and go through life.

I worked with a gorgeous Pit Bull/Staffordshire Bull Terrier cross called Pluto for many years after he was rescued from the street as a seven-week-old pup. He was a great example of a dog whom, as a puppy, you could classify as slightly hard work, trying to escape the garden, pulling on the lead, full of beans, being interested in everything, so the tools we used then were different from the tools I used with him as he got older. As a puppy he would play with anything and everything, and he adored any toy that I was on the end of! As he got older, we used more sniffing games, we added in more food options, we used a heavier ball as he was older, bigger, and able to carry more. The things that remained a lifelong true love for Pluto were balls of all kinds, of varying sizes and varying fabrics, and we continued to use those in his play, his work and throughout every stage of his life. He continued to be rewarded handsomely right up until the end of his life! And what a wonderful dog he was.

The lifetime of a journey with a dog is just incredible. Never be worried about reaching out for help or asking for assistance. That is what people like me, who do this job, are here for. We are here to support you, to help you and to empower you so that you and your dog can live happily side by side.

MENTAL STIMULATION

You know that feeling when you've solved a really diffi-cult problem, or got to the end of a challenging day on the laptop, or finished a book that really made you think? You may not have moved much that day physically, but you feel utterly shattered afterwards because you've worked your brain so hard. You know you've worked hard, and also that you've achieved something. Our dogs need similar levels of mental stimulation in order to feel fulfilled and satisfied. And they get so much of this from play.

I believe giving our dogs proper mental stimulation is enormously important and often overlooked. Owning a dog doesn't mean walking it round the park for an hour and then ignoring it for the rest of the day. Your dog needs interaction and stimulation at other times in the day too.

The ingenuity of dogs always makes me smile. I love how quick and clever they are at figuring out things to do if their needs are not met. Take the Shiba Inu puppy who pulled out every vintage copy of *Vogue* from their owner's shelf to get her attention. Or the Chow Chow who refused to leave the park, because he knew when he got home his owners needed to crack on and work, so all the fun would stop. He cleverly figured out that the fun was all taking place outside of the home and this began to have an effect on how he was viewing inside versus outside.

We all know that dogs need to be walked, to stretch their legs, to run free as a skylark, to sniff and to play. On top of this, I would say mental stimulation is just as important, if not more so than those things. Mental stimulation for your dog is even better if it can be combined with an actual walk and being outside. Or at the very least, in a change of setting, even if that is your front garden, a room you don't use very often or a garage attached to your home. Switching things up is part of the process of making your dog interested and surprised. Just like us, dogs get bored of everything staying the same.

There are always surveys published about the cleverest dog, the smartest breed in the world, etc. I'll be honest, I don't really care which breeds make the top ten of that list, because all dogs still deserve some access to tasks, thinking and challenging play, whether they are Mensa-worthy or not.

There are so many ways that you can start to bring mental stimulation into your dog's life. It will just depend on what your dog likes to do and where their motivation stems from. If your dog has no interest in playing with a ball, and doesn't want to fetch or retrieve, then move on and use other things to stimulate your dog.

For a puppy, I would say that mental stimulation needs to be happening frequently throughout the day, at numerous times. Probably only for up to fifteen minutes at a time, depending on the age of your pup.

For most dogs, you can certainly include a bit of challenging play on one of your walks, plus make time for a morning session and afternoon or evening session too. For some breeds who are designed to 'work' all day, you will need to be doing far, far more than that, in order to keep them satisfied. With a working breed you will need to be carving out huge chunks of your day and evening to create tasks and situations for your dog to solve.

If you have a senior dog, then the mental stimulation will need to increase as the lengths of the walks decrease. Keeping a dog mentally active can help keep its mental capacity in working order. It will also help them to feel included and important, especially if you are starting to introduce younger dogs into the family. Carving out those times for an older dog is still necessary.

Mentally stimulating games and tasks can take many forms:

- chewing activities from short-term to long-lasting ones; vary it up
- hide the chew for them to sniff out and then sit and chow down on
- sniffing games in the garden, the house, the garage
- hide and seek in the house – with people, toys, food, boxes
- using cardboard boxes headed for recycling to make games out of
- scatter feeding using small bits of food, great for working breeds
- scent work to sniff out certain scents that you train them with
- retrieval work
- treat-dispensing toys
- destructive games, where they are allowed to pull something apart, disembowel a toy, rip a tennis ball to shreds, etc.
- agility, indoors or outdoors
- eye-contact games around food and toys

- high levels of obedience training can be incredibly joyful for some breeds
- water play and control around it.

Here are a few of my favourite games to play for mental stimulation:

For puppies and smaller-sized dogs

- Take an empty egg carton and pop a treat into each dip where the egg would normally sit.
- Let your dog pop their nose in and take the treats.
- Repeat this a few times for a couple of days, until they do it automatically.
- Then take a golf ball, fill each dip with a treat again, but this time put the golf ball over the top of one of the treats.
- Let them hoover up all the treats that aren't covered and then let them fathom out how to move the ball to remove the treat.
- Praise them and pet them when they do it.
- Repeat this a few more times until it becomes super-easy for them.
- Now add in another golf ball to cover the treat, so out of six dips in the box, there are two balls covering the treats.
- Keep working up until you have all the dips covered with golf balls.

Do not use golf balls with dogs who could swallow or choke on them. Hence it being a game for smaller dogs.

Ideally we want the dogs to just nudge with their nose or use their paws to pull the balls out of the egg box.

For larger breeds

You can try the same method, but I would use a muffin-baking metal tray, so it is quite deep. And then when you are ready to start covering the treats, use tennis balls. When my Bulldog, Cookie, got really efficient at this game, I started to use heavy cricket balls instead of tennis balls, as they are harder to dislodge! You obviously need to spend some time working up to that.

With both games, you can then begin to keep refilling as around fifteen minutes of this game will be tiring for an adult dog.

GAMES TO PLAY *WITH* YOUR DOG

As I've said earlier, I am not a fan of the idea that 'you must always win' when playing with your dog as otherwise they will feel you're dominant over them. It's rubbish! If you want your dog to continue playing with you, the game should be exactly that, a game, where turns are taken and play is created. If you win every time, your dog will start to disconnect with you, and start to walk away from playing with you. Or if you have a breed who is naturally territorial and possessive, then you run the risk of creating the very behaviours that you do not want – grabbing, guarding and growling. All done to keep you away from the toy, as you have shown them that playing with you is no fun and you always take it.

On the other side of things, the way I work is to try to use play for as much as we can, so that you use play to teach your puppy or dog the manners you would like them to learn. No one wants to sit down and do boring lessons at a desk when they can learn in much more fun formats. The same is true with your dog.

Don't believe that you must have set-aside 'training sessions' in order to form the habits. Every moment, every experience, every adventure is a learning curve for a dog, especially with a puppy.

LEARN HOW YOUR DOG LIKES TO PLAY

I think as a society we still have it very firmly embedded in our heads that all dogs like to play in a certain way. My husband always dreamed of having a dog who likes to play fetch, as none of his childhood dogs were interested. The truth is that every dog is different, and so is the way they like to play. We need to use a dog's natural motivations, personality and preferences to tailor the way we play with them. That way, we can get the very most out of the games, the play and the fun, because the dog wants to engage. We aren't forcing them into it, and we aren't having to cajole them into interacting with us – they should want to partake in what we are suggesting.

If you wanted to use a human example, one of my children adores playing with balls, of any kind: holding them, throwing them, touching them, kicking and catching them. The other child, like me, could not care less about a ball. So if I were a dog that you were trying to motivate with a ball, I'd be the worst partner ever, as I'd just sit there and stare as you lobbed the ball into the sky. I certainly wouldn't be retrieving it and I definitely wouldn't want to chase it.

We also really need to look at your dog's breeding and their natural dispositions as this will help you fathom out 'how' your dog likes to play.

Here is a little experiment you can do with your dog:

Take a ball, ideally a light squidgy tennis ball or lovely sensory rubber one, and show your dog what you have. Sounding excited – not hectic, but just with a fun voice – move it from hand to hand while they watch you. Then just gently roll the ball across the room or in the garden. Don't whack it away too far. It needs to be away from you but not miles away. Now, pay attention: what does your dog do . . . ?

- Run after the ball and pick it up?
- Run after the ball, get to it, but not bother picking it up?
- Pick the ball up and then drop it?
- Pick the ball up and return it to you?
- Pick the ball up and then lie down and try to rip it apart with its teeth?
- Pick the ball up, lie down and chank on it (where

the ball is held in the mouth and pushed down on, repeatedly)?
- Bring the ball back and want you to chase them, trying to tempt you to get hold of the ball?
- None of the above. It just looks at the ball and looks at you!

These are just a few examples of the way that scenario could unfold. None of them is better than another, as they are all ways of playing for different dogs. What it should show you, though, is the bit your dog enjoys doing. For example, if your dog loves the chase of the ball but doesn't want to bring it back, then you know that the chase is the motivator, not the retrieval. It is important to understand these nuances as it enables you to tailor your training, your rewards and how you pick and choose the toys and items that you end up giving your dog.

GROWLING WHEN PLAYING

I've experienced both types of growling while playing – the kind where the dog wants you to keep playing and is trying to get you more involved, and the kind where the dog is telling you that if you come closer they will take your hand off. It's really important that you can distinguish between the two, for very obvious reasons.

. Happy, playful growling should be accompanied by wiggly, waggly body language, invitations to play by trying to get you to chase them or dropping the toy near you.

A playful invitation

They may also lean into you or on to you or flaunt the toy in your face. Barnie, my parents' rescue Bulldog used to do this. He would hold the ball in his mouth, growling, running around, play-bowing, begging to be chased with it, and if you ignored him, he would come into you and try to push himself on to you to get you to get involved. He would make it so there was no way of ignoring him! He certainly did not want the ball to himself; he wanted the engagement, the fun and the frolics. If he took himself to his bed with the ball, I certainly wouldn't follow him, though. I always respect a dog's bed as their space, playful or not. I'd know he was ready to start the game again as he would lie on his bed, then drop the ball just over the edge of the bed so it would then roll and I'd pick it up and off we would go again. I was usually as tired as he was after a session like this!

Guarding growling would generally sound more sinister, and more serious. It is hard to describe in a book! You would be looking for body language that appears tense, that the dog is trying to get away from you, really does not want to share, and wants the item for itself. You may also see eyes that are staring, and you might see 'whale eye', which is where you can see the white parts of their eye. The dog may be alert and ready to lunge, and the tail may be doing a more 'tick-tock' slow movement rather than a playful wiggle. If it has taken the toy to its bed and the dog growls as you so much as walk past, you know that the dog isn't seeing you as a playmate; they are seeing you as a threat. That means the dog may defend the item from you with aggression. This behaviour is not something that you should try to resolve yourself. You will need to work with a behaviourist whom you trust, as you could very quickly make this behaviour much worse if you do the wrong things. Certainly do not reprimand the dog, do not grab the toy from them and do not trick them into giving it to you. A clever dog will learn to trust you even less and this is certainly not a position that you want to be in with a guarding dog.

INTERACTIVE AND INDEPENDENT GAMES

When we look at games, these fall into interactive, where your dog is playing with you or with another dog, or independent, where your dog is playing alone. And every dog should have a mix of both. If your dog is struggling with independence in general, then adding in more games to do on their own can be a gentle starting place to increase their confidence. It should not mean that they only play that way though.

Chasing

Chasing can be an interactive game, as the dog either wants to chase an item or be chased. Be careful with some breeds (e.g. sighthounds, spaniels and Staffies) that this kind of chasing game doesn't become obsessive – as in, it becomes their main focus and you feel you are losing control over that game. You would know the behaviour has become obsessive for your dog if it's the *only* game it wants to play, and with a specific toy. Once you have created an obsessive behaviour, you may never get rid of it. So what can seem a great way to expend energy as a puppy may not be so fun for the rest of their life and can cause havoc with joints and growth plates, as it is lots of stopping, starting, halting and swerving.

Retrieving

This is a great game to teach the idea of 'sharing', but it does take work and a natural motivation. It is also important to select the right kind of toy that your dog 'wants' to hold, pick up and feel in their mouth.

Tugging

I love this game, it is so fun, it is full of energy and can really help a dog release a lot of frustration. Just be aware that this same game can also tip some breeds over the edge. It can make them very hyped, and it can make them lash out if other dogs come over, so you do really need to know your dog and their capabilities. If your dog is as described above, then only play this at home in controlled circumstances or not at all. It may be that this game is too much for them, or it makes them lose focus and unable to listen, which then makes this game no fun for anyone.

Rough and tumble

Usually played with other dogs, but owners will often play like this with a dog too. This should be about play being equally matched, about stopping it before it becomes too much, being able to put an end to a game and to taking it in turns. It is not about control or being bullying. If you notice signs of this, then you should be removing your dog immediately. Play is a rehearsal, it is a way of learning, and you want everything learned to be conducive to the dog you would like to play with in the future. My Bulldog and I used to play rough and tumble together in the evenings, when the kids had gone to bed. It was like she knew they were out of the way and now we could have a roll around. She loved it and it really tired her out. It would only last a few minutes but it was only ever a game that she and I played. And when I finished the game, it was understood that was the end.

Nose games

Games where we teach the dog to use their nose to sniff out items that we hide. This can be interactive or independent, depending on how we play it. For example, I use this a great deal on a walk with Pip, to reward him for not going to say hi to another dog we see. It is interactive because I have taught him two phrases that go with it and as soon as he hears them, he knows what to do and what is going to happen.

'Destructive' games

Many people stop their dogs from pulling toys apart or shredding tennis balls as it is classified as destructive behaviour. I would disagree. This activity is a necessary one for some dogs who are anxious, and some who are determined. It can give a dog a sense of 'completion' to successfully de-squeak a toy, or pull out all the stuffing, though please do oversee these games to make sure they don't swallow anything they shouldn't. I would actively seek out items to give dogs who need to do this and make time for them to solve that task.

Independent games

These are usually more task-related, problem-solving brain games, but we do not need to be there every step of the way.

We do need to be careful that we use the right mix of games for each dog. If you have a highly independent breed like a Welsh Terrier, who I find can be quite solitary dogs, the last thing you want is to be only giving independent games. You will end up with a dog who doesn't view you as being a part of their life for very much at all, except to open doors and perhaps feed them! Whereas if you live with a Cockapoo, you may need to try and get them to be more independent as they struggle so much with any degree of separation.

Free choice vs toys being given to a dog

In addition to this, I do think that each dog (unless they have guarding issues) should have free access to a basket of toys or items that they can select and utilise when their need arises. Many people have this idea that as an owner we should be in charge of absolutely everything that exists in the dog's world, which is a thought I find quite depressing.

A free choice is so that a dog or a puppy gets to choose for themselves, and I use a basket or box that my dog can access whenever he would like. The items I keep in this box are not high value, and they are not items that

I would use as 'motivators'. They are based on Pip's likes and things that I know he won't be obsessed with, so free access is easy.

Pip is a dog who is not high arousal or obsessive, so actually lots of items in the basket would be OK for him. To give you an example of what his basket holds, it has a couple of balls in there (not ones that we use on walks), it also has a random toy that I change every couple of weeks and then it has about three different chewing items, that are long-term chewing items that can't be eaten in one go: an example of this is the split antler.

You can of course rotate the items in the box or basket. The key is to allow the dog to pick and choose. It can also be a way of your dog letting you know they need to do something, or it can be a way of amusing themselves, much like a child getting on and reading a book or doing a puzzle. The idea isn't that you ignore them constantly, but sometimes Pip may fish out an antler to gnaw on for ten minutes before he drops off to sleep. Other times he may pick up a ball and I know it's because he fancies a game. I love the idea of Pip choosing.

For some breeds, you may need to consider the types of items you put in the basket:

- Bull breeds – no rawhide, no chews that they can choke on, as many bull breeds (Frenchie, English Bulldog, Staffy, American Bulldog) will try to chew something up and swallow it in large chunks, so you need to be very cautious of this.
- Spaniels, collies and high-drive working breeds can develop obsessions, so be very cautious around items

like balls, as to live with a dog constantly dropping a ball at your feet can feel relentless. Also bear this in mind when you are creating an obsession in your dog!

• Terriers and Dachshunds love to take apart toys, which isn't a problem so long as your toys can stand up to this. Be cautious about selecting toys that contain squeakers that can be swallowed or horrible fake stuffing that if ingested can really damage the intestines.

Toys for you to control

These should be more the items that you want to use to motivate your dog. This can involve differing treats, food items and toys.

Once you know how your dog plays and what motivates them, you can select the toys accordingly. For example, if you have a sighthound, many of the long, whippy cat toys can be excellent choices, as they can be moved fast and easily. Yet these may not be that interesting to a dog of a different kind.

I also like to have toys that I save or reserve for interactive play together, ones that when I bring them out, the dog knows they are in for some fun. This can take time to build and sometimes we actively have to work to create this anticipation in a dog. It doesn't just magically appear as they have to be taught what different toys mean, and an element of elusivity can help create that interest.

There may also be an element of overlap with some toys. An example is the Kong Ballistic ball, a fabric toy which is held together by Velcro; inside, it has pockets. Within the pockets you can place treats so the dog needs to pull the toy apart with its mouth and then dig out the treats. I keep this item in Pip's free-choice basket, even though he rarely picks it up himself. But I do play with it in two ways. One way is to give it to him in his bed for him to lie down with and pull apart. I would do it this way if he fished it out. On days where I know he may be up for a game, I would hide treats within it, but then I'd hide the toy and send him off to 'find it'. He would then search it out, pick it up and take it back to his bed to dissect. So there are sometimes items that you can utilise for both purposes, depending on what your dog likes to do.

WHY YOU SHOULDN'T TAKE A BALL FROM YOUR DOG'S MOUTH

Often when we start playing with a dog and it picks up the ball or the item we have thrown, it may naturally bring it back to us, or it may go to its bed or safe place to lie down with the item. We then tend to either go to the bed and take the toy from them to throw again, or if they bring it to us and keep it in their mouth to feel, we will take the ball and lob it again.

These first interactions teach a puppy or dog something very simple – when I have something in my mouth, it's going to get taken away, so I should avoid you. If every time you interfere and remove the item, their hard work of going after the toy, collecting it, retrieving it and holding on to it gets ignored, and the reward part – of investigating, discovering and exploring the item – simply vanishes.

Even if you have a dog that is a natural retrieving type or is showing signs of enjoying that kind of game, you still need them to learn that you being around the object is a great thing. You can of course at a later stage start the work on the actual training of a 'retrieve and drop', but if you have a dog who avoids you, doesn't want to play with you and won't come near you with a toy, it is going to make your life way harder. So you need to be focused on encouraging the behaviour you want and then you can train the actual logistics. Don't try to do it the other way around.

So here is how I start. If your dog expresses an interest in picking something up, let them pick it up in their mouth. Stay where you are, don't go after them, don't race them to the object, just sit and observe their natural behaviour.

1. If they tend to bring it and plonk themselves near you with it, just positively praise them and sit and pet them, not touching the toy. Don't interact with the actual item while it's in their mouth. Simply, calmly stroke them. They may sit and mouth on it, and that is fine too.

2. If your dog tends to pick up the item and take it away from you, or tries to distance themselves from you while they have the toy, this is a behaviour you really need to make a concerted effort to work on. They are already seeing you as a threat, and are not naturally drawn to sharing the toy with you – which could develop further if left. So when they pick up the item, do not follow them. Just observe where they go to with the toy.

The next time you throw the item, make sure you are sitting relatively near to the area they took it back to the previous time; not right next to it but close by. This is so that as they turn around to trot back to the allocated safe space, you can praise them, cheer them on a bit, sound pleased for them, but don't reach out to touch them. If they return to their bed and not to you, or they come nearer to you, still don't grab the toy. Continue to sound happy for them and say, 'What have you got?' or similar, so it sounds like an excited question, and if they come closer just pet their body gently, while still sounding happy. You are simply trying to change their association with what it means to pick up an item, and that they do not need to feel threatened by your presence. Spend quite a bit of time – as in days and weeks – doing this, until you start to see that your dog instinctively picks the ball up, trots back to you and either drops it or they lie next to you with it, happily being petted.

You do also need to consider whether the item you are using to throw is too much for them, too stimulating, or too tempting to chew or teethe on. For example, if you have a dog who is teething a great deal and you are throwing a rubber toy, you will find it hard to get the dog to release the toy, as the material is an extremely satisfying sensation for the dog to hold on to and teethe on. So do remember that the material and the item will affect the dog's abilities to learn. I am all for the idea of having differing toys, items, objects for different purposes – you just need to sit and figure out which things work for which purpose.

As an example, for many clients, we work out the array of balls a dog may enjoy and then we rate them. We then use that rating to figure out how to use them and when. The sky is the limit when it comes to mental stimulation for you and your dog. Rather than slavishly working through the suggestions above one by one, it is more about figuring out the kinds of things your dog enjoys and using that to your advantage. On days when perhaps it's raining and I have both children at home, getting them to hold an end of a broom each while we teach our dog Pip to learn to jump over it is tiring for all of us!

You may also want to create a kind of toy library for your dog. Rather than buy new toys all the time, just hide several toys for weeks or months, then bring them out again. Your dog will be as excited by the return of some old toys as by the brand-new ones.

Your dog should learn games that it can play with you, and ones it can play alone. Both types of play are important for a dog. Ideally you would like them to enjoy playing with you, but equally sometimes we do need them to get on and do something we have provided them with, alone.

Very often owners can be so caught up in getting their dog or puppy to play alone that the dog stops seeing them as a play partner. I do understand why it happens, but we need to guard against this, as then your dog will look to others, usually dogs, as the play partner and then this can in turn increase the dog focus and them wanting to get away from you.

This is especially true of dogs I see in the park who get out of the house and then want to get as far away from their owner as possible – as they want to play. And they see that chase, that wrestling, all coming from other dogs rather than the people they live with.

There will of course be times we need our dogs to occupy themselves, perhaps when they are teething, to allow us to make a work phone call or while bathing the children, which might be with a treat-dispensing toy or a chew. But try not to constantly just offer independent play options. I suggest actively offering a balance of games, toys and exercises which are a combination of interaction and independence. Make sure that across a day you have played with your dog and been a source of fun, but equally provided some options for your dog to work on alone such as a chew stick or a treat-dispensing toy.

CHAPTER FIFTEEN

What Your Dog Wants You to Know about Kids

Growing up with a dog can be an amazing experience for a child, and there are many dogs who adore children. Sadly there are also many dogs who are afraid of kids, and whose interactions with them have been frightening or painful. My first recommendation is that no baby or small child should ever be left alone with a dog. You need to monitor both the child's behaviour and the dog's – you do not want to miss any of those 'green' signals from a dog in the presence of a child.

Small children are still learning about social cues from humans. Their ability to read others' emotions can be hard, so it is unrealistic to imagine that they will naturally know how to behave around a dog or to interpret its behaviour. In addition, many children are never taught to respect the boundaries a dog needs, and this can have a catastrophic impact.

In my experience, there are six reasons why a dog will end up biting a child. The reason this bite is often on a child's face is due to the relative heights of the dog and the child, and the position kids will put their faces in to greet or see a dog.

1. The child didn't let the dog disconnect. If you recall, in the traffic-light system I have laid out, disconnection is one of the first behaviours a dog will offer to leave a situation it doesn't like. Imagine a dog lying on the sofa, asleep, when a child decides it too would like to sit on the sofa, next to the resting dog. The dog feels uncomfortable or doesn't feel like being petted, so it moves to the other end of the sofa. The child shifts along with it, so the dog hops down and goes and lies splat on the floor by the sofa. The child then plonks themselves on the floor next to the dog. Now the dog goes and gets under the kitchen table, and the child moves the chair to either continue to pet it or to get to it. The dog, in a two-minute interaction, has learned that disconnection does not work. If this behaviour is then repeated numerous times a day, a few times a week, then very soon there is going to be an amber incident, which will lead to a red-zone problem. And that child will end up being bitten.

2. The dog was disturbed when it was sleeping. All puppies and dogs require sleep, which is crucial for all of our sanity, wellbeing and biological functions. Like us, dogs have varying stages of sleep. When they go into a deep state of sleep, being disturbed can truly shock them, like it would shock you if you were shaken awake at 3 a.m. If a child disturbs a dog in a deep sleep, by kissing it on the face or trying to hug it,

the mouth and teeth will be the first thing to make contact with that child's skin.

3. The dog is expected to have no boundaries. I think the main thing to remember with this point is that if there is respect, personal space and very clearly defined boundaries between a child and a dog, that relationship can fully blossom. Stair gates are brilliant for enforcing those boundaries and I wholeheartedly encourage their use. Many images on social media depict a dog and child together, the dog being leaned upon, sat on, hugged around the neck, having their mouth played with, as if the dog should simply tolerate this kind of interaction. We do have to remember that our dogs are still animals, with teeth capable of pulling meat off a bone. They have predatory behaviours that we as humans have bred into them for thousands of years. They are not simply a walking, playing life-sized toy of a teddy bear here to amuse and satisfy our children's desires.

4. A dog should have respect shown towards it. A child should understand that a dog is not a toy; it has feelings, emotions, fears and pain thresholds, and to breach any of those things may create a reaction you do not like. Whether it's your child or a family member's children, if boundaries cannot be adhered to or put into place, the dog and the child should not be allowed to mix. I take prevention very seriously and in some instances will just put my dog upstairs, away from other children visiting the home, if I don't think they are capable of listening, following what I ask, or I just don't want to think about what the

dog and the children are doing. Prevention is always better than cure.

5. Persisting with something the dog dislikes. This could be a baby pulling at their fur, as the baby's ability to stroke has not developed yet. It could be the pulling of a tail, grabbing of ears, or being grabbed from behind while they are eating. If things keep being done to them, over and over again, a dog will be left with no choice but to snap. And the result of the dog snapping is that immediately that baby will be scooped up and whisked away. So the dog learns that snapping created the exact desirable effect and gets rid of the child. Please don't leave it to get to that point. If you see a friend's dog and children heading down this path, don't be too scared to offend by saying something. Direct them to this part of my book, as you could be preventing a child being bitten and needing plastic surgery and a dog being put to sleep. That is how serious the consequences could be, if just left alone.

6. Shock or pain can be a factor. Sometimes a dog can be shocked and respond without thinking, in the same way we would in that moment. A dog was recently found by police tethered up in the snow, with sores all over his body and appalling ear infections in both ears, and when the police officer went to pick the dog up, it bit them. This poor dog ended up having to have both ear canals removed because of the severity of pain and damage from the ear infections. This highlights the level of pain the dog was in. The dog was still given a chance of being rehomed.

7. A genuine accident. Perhaps a dog is lying in the way and someone stumbles and falls on to its tail. This happened to a client who was on a train with their dog. They hadn't realised their dog was lying in the train aisle, a child went past and trod on the dog's tail, by accident, and the dog nipped the child's ankle. My son when he was younger also did something similar with a large-breed dog.

The key to all of these situations is that we as the parents and/or dog owners have control over five out of seven of these reasons, which stacks up to pretty good odds of preventing children being bitten.

It is my belief that as well as dog owners training and teaching their dog, parents must also teach reciprocal respect of animals. Even if you do not plan to ever own a dog, we all have to share spaces, parks and paths, and mutual respect and tolerance are really a key factor in all of this. It is not acceptable to expect random, unknown dogs, in fact even dogs you know very well, to just handle or desire the attentions of your child. When I'm walking my dog, I often have parents walk towards me and say, 'Oh, they love dogs,' which is wonderful, as do I. In order to make that love safe, reciprocal and respectful, we must then be teaching children to not simply walk up to and touch each dog they see. We have to remember that these are still living, moving, breathing, unpredictable animals with emotions and feelings.

WHAT SHOULD WE BE TEACHING OUR DOGS TO DO AROUND CHILDREN?

- An auto 'sit' can be useful, to avoid jumping up. (Unless your dog is scared of children, in which case making them sit is less than ideal.)
- To walk away if they dislike something.
- Not to run up into children.
- To be able to be on a lead calmly and walk past kids.
- That if they do not like children, or have a fear of them, we will leave them at home to rest instead of taking them into busy spaces where it is an uncontrollable variable and venue.
- To be able to take a treat from the ground, recommended as a way for unknown children or strangers to give treats, so that we avoid snatching, kids pulling hands away, or over-excitement from kids and dogs.
- To accept being behind a baby gate or to be able to be separated and happily accept it. This is very important in my eyes.

WHAT SHOULD WE BE TEACHING OUR CHILDREN AROUND DOGS?

- Never touch a dog who is eating or drinking.
- If a dog is not interested in you, walk away.
- If a dog is asleep, you do not touch it.
- Never get in with or touch a dog in a crate, pen or its bed.

- Not to hug a dog or kiss it in the face.
- Avoid pulling things from a dog's mouth.
- That over-excitement, running and screaming will arouse a dog.
- It isn't acceptable to run into a dog in a pub, a park, or on the street.
- If you wouldn't want it done to you, you don't do it to a dog, e.g. putting Lego in an ear, pulling at hair.
- To never sit on a dog.
- To not follow dogs.
- To not shout or scream at dogs.

CHAPTER SIXTEEN

What Your Dog Wants You to Know about Food

At a conservative estimate, there are over 250 brands of dog food available in the UK. It's not surprising that many owners are confused about the best way to feed their dog, and it's one of the things I get asked about often by clients. Feeding a dog needn't be madly complicated if you stick to one basic principle, and that is that your dog has evolved to eat fresh food and the closer you get to that, the better. No matter how 'nutritionally complete' or 'organic' the dog kibble is, no dog desires to eat nothing but biscuits day in, day out – just like no human could be sustained purely on breakfast cereal.

In terms of what to feed, this will vary according to where you live, your budget, your dog, what you have available, etc. For me, the main thing to keep in your mind is that your dog is meant to eat fresh food – meat, vegetables, fruits and a small amount of carbohydrates. Fresh food is absolutely fundamental in my mind and I urge you to ensure your dog is not just being fed the same boring kibble day in, day out.

It is also worth mentioning that what works for one dog may not work for another. Just because your mum or your friend fed their dog something doesn't mean it will work for your dog.

In the last decade, some truly brilliant independent food companies have begun selling excellent fresh, cooked, raw and dehydrated options. You will need to weigh up the options according to your budget and where your priorities lie, but I would urge you to buy the best quality you can afford. In my opinion, you won't source the best options in a supermarket set-up. They will stock the big companies' products but not necessarily the higher-quality, most nutritious options.

There are many great vets out there who will give great dog-feeding advice, but it is worth bearing in mind that much of the nutrition training given to veterinary students is funded by the major dog-food companies.

If your dog has particular food or health issues, it would be worth seeking out a dog nutritionist, though do ensure they are independent, as many brands have nutritionists that they pay or keep on a retainer. I have a professional whom I work alongside and whom I put my clients in touch with, as her expertise in this field far exceeds mine. This part of the book is just the tip of the iceberg when it comes to dog nutrition, but hopefully these pages have opened your eyes enough to begin exploring it in much more depth.

I've highlighted some of the main feeding options below, to help you narrow down the best way to feed your dog. I have no paid alliances with any food brands, so my opinions are purely that, not based on relationships with particular brands or me being paid to highlight something. I do occasionally do social media ads for certain treats that I like using, but even that isn't a regular occurrence.

Like humans, every dog will be different. What one dog tolerates or loves to eat, another may not. So pay attention. If your dog leaves half its food, or isn't interested in eating it, then you may need to think again. And if your dog loses its appetite, please always seek a vet's opinion, as it may be a sign of a more serious issue. It can also just be down to the fact that the dog knows there are better options out there and they want them, but it's always best to check.

DRY FOOD, AKA KIBBLE

Dry food was created to offer more convenience for dog owners, rather than what is best for their dogs. Even the premium, organic brands go through the process of all raw ingredients being extruded to form a kind of dough, which is then exposed to heat or steam to cook it at a minimum of 180 degrees. The dough is then pushed through a tube, cut into pieces and any remaining moisture is sucked out of the food by going underneath a heavy-duty dryer. From there, the pellets are sprayed with animal fat, salt and flavourings to make the food more appealing to any dog taking a sniff. My opinion: this food was not created as a species-relevant diet, it was created to make profit and maximise on the by-products of other industries. A dog's stomach is not designed to digest this kind of product for every meal.

Pros: it is easy to feed; it has a long shelf life; it can be cheaper.

Cons: it is not nutritionally dense; no dog was designed to eat a dry food day in and day out.

TINNED OR WET FOOD

These are made by putting raw foods into tins or plastic trays and the foodstuffs are then cooked within the vessel itself. These kinds of foods typically contain fewer synthetic preservatives than kibble as the airtight, tinned containers do this job more effectively. My opinion: this sector can vary enormously, so it is impossible to make a statement about them generically, as what each brand uses differs significantly. The ingredient list will be the most important thing that you look at and understand. Be very cautious about the 'meat and animal derivatives' listed in many of these products. Brands using actual 'meat' and ingredients that you are able to identify are the most favourable.

Pros: usually have more meat and less carbohydrates than kibble; can be more digestible and palatable.

Cons: many brands can hide a multitude of sins by putting pretend meat products in gravy, etc.

RAW FOOD

This is composed of meat, organs and animal products such as ground raw meaty bones. The raw feeding brands take these raw ingredients and usually put them through an industrial-sized mincer or grinder, to make it into a more accessible food for owners to store and serve. My opinion: a highly nutritious way of feeding your dog, there are many brands who make it and deliver it frozen to your door. Many vets will advise it is a dangerous way of feeding your dog, though research and many nutritionists would disagree with this. You can also explore making your own raw-food recipes.

Pros: you can offer great variety easily; it can be a relevant way to feed, whatever your budget.

Cons: some dislike the idea of feeding raw meat; needing to have extra freezer or fridge space available.

DEHYDRATED FOOD

This is a relatively new way of feeding and offers an easier way to feed but with more nutrients being retained in the processing of the food. It is essentially where the raw food has undergone air- or freeze-drying. This makes it more ready to use than raw food. Also using these methods of air/freeze-drying means it retains much of its nutrients. My opinion: it can be a good option if you need to feed one meal out and about or out of the home. You can also mix it with raw or cooked food.

Pros: more nutrient dense than dry food; easy to transport and carry around; maintains its nutrient profile.

Cons: it can feel less palatable to some dogs; some you have to mix with water to rehydrate them.

COOKED FOOD

More people are choosing to cook for their own dogs than ever before. There are also now brands cooking the food and delivering to homes in frozen containers, ready to be defrosted. My opinion: for a dog who doesn't like to eat raw, this can be a nutritional way of feeding. Or if you don't feel comfortable feeding raw, this is an excellent option.

Pros: can be fed cold or heated up; nutritious; generally fresh ingredients; easy way to feed.

Cons: you need to either have time to cook the food yourself, or fridge and freezer space to hold the food; cheap fillers like lentils can still be added to the big-brand products, so do assess the ingredients list.

If you would like to transition your dog from one type of feeding on to another food, do be aware that sometimes the change can unsettle a dog's stomach. I would suggest making the transition slowly and steadily: don't rush it. You want your dog to be able to tolerate and enjoy the new food, so spend a good seven to ten days transitioning your dog to a new diet. I always recommend beginning with the breakfast meal, as it means you have all day with your dog to observe any issues. If, for example, you were moving your dog from a dry, kibble-based diet to a fresher diet, I would suggest starting to introduce one teaspoon of the new fresh diet into the dry kibble for breakfast. Do that for a couple of days in the breakfast meal. If that is tolerated for two days, then on day three I would add two teaspoons of fresh food and remove two teaspoons of the kibble. And continue like this with the breakfast meal until the whole thing is the new diet. Provided this works, then you can continue with the same format for the lunch and supper meals.

Dog-food ingredients

When it comes to the ingredients you want to see in your dog's food, they should be ingredients you recognise, in significant quantities. Ingredients are always listed by volume first, so you want to see whole meat as the first ingredient. Here is the ingredients list from an independent fresh-food brand that does home-cooked food, delivered frozen:

Beef (Mince, Heart, Liver), Spinach (12.9%), Squash (8%), Carrot, Apple (5%), Mushroom, Salmon Oil, Olive Oil, Parsley, Monocalcium Phosphate, Brewers' Yeast, Chia Seeds, Kelp, Minerals and Turmeric.

I would be happy to feed this to my dog.

By contrast, here's an ingredients list from a 'prescription' diet from a big corporation:

Brewers' rice, chicken by-product meal, oat groats, wheat, corn gluten meal, chicken fat, natural flavors, dried plain beet pulp, fish oil, calcium carbonate, vegetable oil, potassium chloride, salt, monocalcium phosphate, choline chloride, hydrolyzed yeast, vitamins [DL-alpha tocopherol acetate (source of vitamin E), L-ascorbyl-2-polyphosphate (source of vitamin C), biotin, D-calcium pantothenate, vitamin A acetate, niacin supplement, pyridoxine hydrochloride (vitamin B6), thiamine mononitrate (vitamin B1), vitamin B12 supplement, riboflavin supplement, vitamin D3 supplement, folic acid], L-lysine, trace minerals [zinc proteinate, zinc oxide, ferrous sulfate, manganese proteinate, manganous oxide, copper sulfate, calcium iodate, sodium selenite, copper proteinate], magnesium oxide, rosemary extract, preserved with mixed tocopherols and citric acid.

The first ingredient in the prescription diet is a cheap filler: the broken and fragmented bits of rice that are surplus to requirement for other foods or dishes. Some have described this as the sweepings off the floor, as it previously would have been discarded and got rid of. The promised 'meat' is chicken by-product meal – this is the leftovers of the chicken: necks, feet and undeveloped eggs that are then ground down into meal. This certainly isn't high-quality meat. While it is good to use all of the carcass, if you look at the list above, this is the second main ingredient of the prescription diet. Which means that by-product is mostly what your dog will be eating. And the price ticket attached to it will not reflect the low-level quality of the ingredients.

As dog ownership soars and we care for our pups, the dog-food industry is now a juggernaut of cash. In theory it is great that people want to feed their dogs well. If only the big players were creating food worthy of our best friends. Instead, a great deal of time and cash is being put into creating foods that use the cheapest ingredients with the best mark-up – not what is nutritionally best for the dog.

It is worth knowing that in the UK, three corporations own 90 per cent of all pet-food sales. These are Mars, Nestlé and Colgate-Palmolive. This should give you some indication of the quality you can expect. They possess huge budgets to market their food to you and your dog, to tempt you into feeding it one of their brands without often knowing or realising that the food is made by a gigantic corporation.

The manufacturers have a huge amount of control over what we as the public understand and the terms that are used on food, so it's essential that you have an understanding of the terms used before you spend money on low-quality food for your pet.

Watch out for the following terms on pet food:

'Complete food'. The definition of a 'complete food' is one that meets a dog's daily nutritional needs. However, these nutritional guidelines are set by the European Pet Food Industry Federation (FEDIAF), whose other job is to represent the interests of European pet-food manufacturers. In other words, the pet-food manufacturers are setting their own rules.

Hypoallergenic. A term that should mean it won't trigger allergic reactions. It's not, as many people seem to think, a marker of quality. Food can be hypoallergenic and still contain fillers and other ingredients that aren't nutrient dense.

Natural. Implies that the ingredients could be found in nature, but again this does not mean it's good quality. A pig's ear is natural, but if it's been dipped in a chemical solution, you shouldn't be feeding it to your dog.

Prescription diet. A marketing term created by the likes of Hill's and Royal Canin. I don't feel this is necessary for any dog; the only exception is some for medical issues – for example, with kidney failure.

Beet pulp. A product used to put fibre into a dog's diet, of very limited nutritional value.

Gluten meal. Sometimes listed as maize meal or corn meal, used as an even cheaper way to add protein into a dog food. However, many dogs cannot digest or utilise this product and if more protein was needed, actual meat would be far more preferable.

Natural flavours. This term can be used to describe any product that is an extract from any food where its main function is for flavour rather than nutrition. This could

THE BOOK YOUR DOG WISHES YOU WOULD READ

be grains that have been soaked or it could be a broth. The manufacturer does not need to state the specifics of the flavour. Some brands will spray the food at the end stages of processing to make the food appear more palatable.

Meat and animal derivatives. According to European law, 'meat and animal derivatives' is classified as 'all the fleshy parts of slaughtered warm-blooded land animals, fresh or preserved by appropriate treatment, and all products and derivatives of the processing of the carcass or parts of the carcass of warm-blooded land animals'. The problem is that the term is so very vague, so there really is no way of knowing what this does or does not include in term of the actual protein, the parts and the quality of it.

Tocopherols. A naturally occurring preservative.

Bone meal. Ground-up bone, which can be beneficial for a calcium source but the manufacturers do not need to list the source of the bone meal. So if your dog were intolerant or allergic to chicken and the bone meal used was from chickens, this would be problematic, yet you would not know about it.

Freshly prepared meat. Means a meat slurry or paste that although it began life as meat has since gone through five separate processes – mechanical separation, grinding, pasteurisation (usually done using heat), separation and finally concentration. I don't mind this in treats, but for daily meals . . . not so much.

Fresh meat. It should be exactly that, a high-quality ingredient that is nutritious for a dog to eat.

Loaf. This is where a variety of ingredients are cooked into a loaf, then sliced up and coated in a gravy or jelly. Very often this type of food is almost entirely made up of cereals along with meat and animal derivatives. In one example I looked at, only 4 per cent was listed as being from an animal protein, despite it being labelled as a 'chicken loaf'.

Fabricated meat. This is a term that you will never see appear on a label, but it doesn't mean that it's not in your dog's food. Many of the loaf-style, meaty-cuts type foods may actually be vegetable proteins that are being used to fabricate beef or chicken products. It would seem that the pet-food industry is not required to tell consumers if the chunks of meat are actual meat or fabricated.

Country of Origin

If you take a walk around your local larger pet store, you will find it rather easy to find tins, bags and other items that in tiny lettering state that the food is made in China, Poland or Thailand. The main reason I have an issue with pet food made in China is down to their history of using chemicals, and product recalls that caused the deaths of dogs who suffered from eating these treats and food.

It is also worth noting that before 2018 there were no

governing regulations for the production of dog food in China. Although some guidelines have been implemented, it is still unclear how these are being policed and enforced. For other countries, we do need to pay attention to their welfare and animal husbandry records.

I try to avoid products from Poland and Thailand as their standards of animal husbandry are not up to UK standards, and that concerns me. It is becoming harder to find products not made in these countries.

It is legally possible for dog foods and treats to be listed as made in the UK when some of the ingredients were pre-mixed in other countries. So the safest way to ensure your dog's health is to look for treats with as few ingredients and preservatives as possible.

Which is why my main advice would be to seek out an independent food maker, of which there are some amazing ones, using locally sourced and incredible ingredients. They will each be happy to relay their sourcing information, where every ingredient comes from, country of origin and so forth, and you can literally call them up to discuss the details so that you can feel reassured about what you are choosing.

If all else fails, you can of course return to the way of feeding my grandpa, who was a farmer, used – which was to feed the dogs the scraps from the table, so that he knew exactly what each dog was eating, and this is easy enough to do once you know the format of what you should be feeding. In order to do this properly, you will need to pay a canine nutritionist to go through this with you, to make sure you do it safely.

All in all, the main thing to remember is that the power

is in your hands. Do not feel pushed into feeding your dog anything. You must consider what feels right for your dog, what you can afford and aim to feed the best foodstuff that you are able.

CHEWS AND TREATS

We all rely on these types of items every single day if we have a dog in our life, and we actively search out delicious options to tempt our dog, to reward training and to encourage them through life. So it is important that we also look at what we are dishing out every day.

Treats can be concocted using terrible ingredients, predominantly cereals or fillers such as wheat, corn and maize. As far as you can, you should really try to use treats that are as natural as possible – as in, the ingredients are once again items you recognise, such as sweet potato, chicken meat, peas, etc.

The same terms and names apply to treats as they do to food, so you need to be as cautious as you would be with the food you are now going to be feeding.

Many of the chews that are coming on to the market are full of derivatives of some kind or another, making claims about teeth cleaning and oral care, yet they are also stuffed full of sugar, salt and flavourings. Do not accept the claims as truth: you still need to go through the list with a fine toothcomb before giving them to your dog.

Sadly, the same is true of some of the more 'natural' animal parts being used as a teething or chew item – a prime example is that of the pig's ear. When you see the body parts that are a dark brown colour or even a red colour, this is where the item has been dipped in a fat solution, to preserve it and to stop it from going rotten. This same fat may preserve the ear, but it will likely cause your dog to have an upset stomach.

If your dog has a known intolerance or allergy (my Bulldog used to not be able to tolerate any kind of cooked chicken), then you do also need to make sure your treats do not contain any of those triggering ingredients. This is the perfect example: 'real meaty treats with beef – beef 50%, pork 45%'. The treat is practically half pork, a totally different protein from the one labelled on the front, and the pork does not have to be mentioned on the front of the packet. So if you were just browsing in a store and were looking for pure beef-based treats, you would be incorrect to assume that a beef treat was just made up of beef!

WHY I'M NOT A HUGE FAN OF SLOW-FEEDING BOWLS

If you have a dog who is eating like a gannet, quickly and without chewing, you may be recommended a 'slow-feeding bowl', which makes a dog work harder to access its food. This food-gulping type of behaviour is actually indicative of either panic around food (perhaps they have been starved previously), a dog who isn't absorbing nutrients properly (hence the need to scoff out of hunger), or a general feeling of threat around food (so it needs to disappear as quickly as possible). None of the reasons behind swallowing food this quickly are healthy ones that we want to encourage. Instead, we want to be working towards solving them and helping the dog calm down.

I don't believe in using these kinds of bowls as I actually feel it is cruel to make a dog who is worried or anxious about food work even harder to get it. All we are doing is reinforcing that fear around food. It doesn't actually solve the issue. You will note that it doesn't stop the rushing, it makes them more driven, more hyped, as they can now smell and see the food but it's going to take it longer to get it into their body.

For some dogs, it can also propel the journey for resource guarding, i.e. getting aggressively protective of its food, as it builds frustration and leads to the dog's adrenaline being raised. They may become snappier as they cannot physically reach the food they are so desperate for, which makes me feel sad.

What we should actually be ensuring is that the food they are being fed is extremely high quality, fresh and nutrient dense. We should be supporting them with supplements rather than just making it harder to acquire food. I'd also be introducing more than three meals per day, so that the dog's appetite is kept at bay and they don't reach a point of being really hungry, which can then create the panic around the food. Very often, I've found that these dogs are also the ones who struggle to gain weight, that they process food very quickly, and they are doing more eliminations per day than I'd expect, which all indicates that they aren't actually taking from the food what they should be.

A Pointer-cross dog from a rehoming charity that a lovely client took on was one of the worst starvation cases the charity had ever seen. He was skeletal. So a huge amount of work had to be done to manage his food obsessions. He actually was never aggressive around food, just obsessed. It took many months of work to get the supplementation right, and the diet and portions correct, to make sure he had a constant feeling of fullness before we could even begin to think about teaching any manners around food. Don't run before you can walk and don't add in unnecessary stress where it isn't needed.

CHAPTER SEVENTEEN

What Your Dog Wants You to Know about Dog Walkers, Daycare and Kennels

It can feel like a big deal finding the right person or people to look after your dog when you can't, whether that's for a day, a weekend or a more regular arrangement to cover times when you're at work. I encourage my clients to choose a walker based on their dog's particular desires, needs and abilities. For example, if you have a dog who is afraid of children, you will want to ensure that your dog walker is aware of this and able to accommodate it, rather than thrusting your dog into a busy family home and hoping it will be OK.

Finding the right person will take more than a Google search to locate the one nearest to you.

When you find a brilliant walker to become part of your dog's life, it can feel such a relief to have someone else that you can rely on and who will look after your dog when you are unable. I encourage all of my clients to remember that a dog walker's main role is to safely, constructively and positively exercise your dog when you are not around. It is not fair, or realistic, to place too many expectations on daycare or a dog walker. They would, hopefully, be able to work with you on any issues your dog may have, but they are not there to solve all of your dog's behavioural problems.

It is worth mentioning that some of the dogs I work with as a behaviourist have had issues created or exacerbated by a walker or a daycare who simply had no idea what they were doing. As more providers pop up, the more wary and selective you need to be in choosing whom you trust with your dog. If you are going to be giving someone keys to your home, and the responsibility of caring for your family member, you really need to trust them and believe in them.

WHAT YOU ARE LOOKING FOR IN A DOG WALKER OR DAYCARE:

- That they are insured.
- That they have experience in working with dogs: find out exactly what this means! Don't feel afraid to ask about all the carers within the daycare – many daycare staff will move on quickly and there can be a high turnover, so you do want to know how experienced their current staff are.
- They can offer you solo walks to begin with, to get to know your dog and you before they embark on group walks.
- To understand how they mix and match the dogs in their walking groups: location or size of dog should not be the overriding reason.
- To know the number of dogs they walk and where

they walk them, so that you can observe them out and about.

- What is the ratio of people to dogs in walking/daycare settings? I'd want to see something like one person for every four to five dogs.
- To find out the exact dogs yours may be going out with. I'd want to know about them individually – as they may not be right for your dog.
- Understanding their methods: do they say one thing and do another? People can say anything on a website, so you need to see first hand.
- To be given detailed feedback at the end of each day or walk via email, WhatsApp, text or in person.

WHAT YOU DON'T WANT IN A DOG WALKER OR DAYCARE:

- Vast operations with heaps of dogs and no personal attention.
- Dogs spending huge amounts of time in a van.
- People who use dominance techniques.
- Inexperienced people with unreasonable expectations.
- Those who spend more time on their social media than they do with your dog.
- Those who are walking dogs according to size or simply age.
- I really am not a fan of puppy daycares. In my experience, they can create issues for puppies such as bullying and intimidation between pups.

By choosing and selecting a daycare or walker, you are choosing someone who is going to influence your dog day in and day out. You need to feel confident in what they are doing. I've seen every trick under the sun from unscrupulous dog walkers, from lying about length of walks, to dogs being bullied and attacked within a walking group and owners being lied to about how it happened, and even dogs escaping vans and being run over. I've had a full-on argument with a daycare which 'specialised in daycare for puppies' yet were absolutely clueless about the handling of puppies during a heatwave and were more focused on taking photos of the puppies wearing crowns underneath a tree.

In my experience, these unscrupulous dog carers are not the majority, but you do need to go out on a walk with the person without your dog in tow before you sign your dog up for their care. Then you need to trial your dog and you need to be present before you even consider a trial of them walking your dog for you. If there is anything you feel in your gut that doesn't feel right, you keep on searching. I once met a walker who was so lovely, but a particular dog in the group that mine would have had to go out with was a real bully and I just knew the dynamic would not be a good one. Trust your instincts and don't always rely on other people's recommendations, as we all have different dogs.

KENNELS

As I said in the earlier chapter about taking on a rescue dog, kennels can be a very overwhelming experience for a dog. Unless your dog is used to kennels – for example, a working dog who is kept in a kennel – it would not be my first choice for when you go away. A family dog, who is used to a home, is likely to be highly stressed when isolated in a kennel environment, even if it's plush and heated. If at all possible, I would much prefer you to find a home environment such as a dog-sitter over kennels. They should be a last resort.

I have come across kennels that claim someone will be with your dog all the time, but in my experience this is not the case, and you should not rely on this. I'd want to know exactly what their definition of this is, as 'staffing' can mean someone just walking around the perimeter of a fence rather than actually engaging with your dog.

CHAPTER EIGHTEEN

What Your Dog Wants You to Know About What It Wears

Choosing your dog's accessories is so much more than a fashion decision! I know how tempting it is to select a collar and lead based on what looks good, or seems attractive, but when I look around the park I sometimes wince at the decisions that have been made in the interests of the owner rather than the dog.

Your dog knows nothing about the law, obviously, but it's worth you knowing as an owner that collars with an ID tag are mandatory in most countries. In the UK there is a £5,000 fine if your dog isn't wearing a collar and tag in a public place.

So make sure you have a collar that will stay on, and a tag which has your mobile phone number and your house number and postcode. If you have a working dog you don't want it to wear a tag for fear of injury, but you can have this information engraved on the collar buckle instead, or sewn on to fabric collars.

I do not advise having your dog's name on its tag. It gives someone an advantage if they are trying to steal your dog. If your dog reacts to its name, it may respond to anyone who calls it.

Collars can vary hugely in quality and price and style, so I'd suggest a few things to bear in mind when making your selection:

Puppy collars

A collar for a puppy should initially be lightweight, thin and not overbearing. It's not a real collar for use outside; it's intended just to get them used to the feeling of wearing one. Lots of breeders start using collars made of coloured paper so they can tell the puppies apart, but this is also a great introduction for the puppies to get used to wearing something around their necks from early on. Some breeds, like Shiba Inus, can be highly touch sensitive, so be sure to select the most delicate, lightweight option to start with.

Hound collars

These specialist wide leather collars need to be used on longer-necked dogs, such as whippets and greyhounds, to make sure any pressure on the collar is evenly distributed across the neck.

Buckle collars

For heavier, more powerful breeds, I prefer to make sure the collar is securely fitted with a metal buckle. These dogs are strong and will pull, so be cautious with plastic buckles as they can't withstand the same pull pressure.

Choke chains

These metal chain collars, which tighten around a dog's neck as it pulls, were very much a 1980s phenomenon that has thankfully fallen out of favour. Choking your dog is never a good idea.

Prong collar

This is a collar with metal spikes on the inside of the collar, so that when the dog pulls, the prongs dig into the fur and throat. Supposedly this stops a dog from pulling, but for obvious reasons I am not a fan. They are unnecessary and cruel. There are so many other options available to you if you are struggling with lead walking that much.

Head collar

These are fastened around the dog's muzzle and clipped under the chin. They are often used on giant breeds or dogs that people find hard to loose-lead train, because it means the dog can't put their full body weight behind pulling as it can do with a neck collar or harness. While I do understand lead training can be laborious and time-intensive, it can be worth it. However, I'd also rather you walked your dog in a head collar and it actually got walked than it not being walked because you feel you cannot safely control your dog on a regular collar and lead. Do bear this factor in mind too when you are considering taking on an 80-kilo St Bernard, as this will need to be a big focus of your training right from the word go.

Muzzle

I think a muzzle is a brilliant piece of equipment for dogs who can be aggressive, who have a history of using their teeth or who scavenge. People are often scared to use them, but it is the responsible thing to do if you have a reactive dog. It can make walks much more relaxing if people can visibly see that they should perhaps give your dog a bit more space. Do make sure you use a properly fitting basket muzzle that your dog can drink through, take treats through and if it were to vomit, could do so. Never ever be tempted to use the muzzles that slip over a dog's face and stop them opening their mouth: these are inhumane and vile.

In order to teach a dog to accept a muzzle, you will need to do extensive desensitisation work with the muzzle. Initially I'd pair the muzzle with something positive which the dog enjoys, such as food or games. Put a treat in the muzzle so that the dog reaches in for a treat. It's not usually an issue for a dog to put its face into a muzzle, but they often don't like it once you fasten the muzzle, so this may take a while. Do work with a behaviourist on this if you are concerned. I often teach puppies to use a muzzle before it is needed, so that we create an early positive association with them, related to taking treats and being fed. This is so that if, later on in life, you need to start using them, you have a great foundation to build from.

Harnesses

If you prefer a harness that fastens around your dog's body rather than its neck, there are an array of options open to you. I find that many clients buy them in order to solve a pulling problem, but they're not a magic solution. Wearing a harness will reduce pressure on the dog's neck, it may help prevent injuries and, if you are using a long line in the park, you must attach it to a well-fitting harness. I am seeing more and more harnesses being used where you can attach Velcro patches to the outside of it, e.g. 'nervous dog'/'friendly dog', etc. In theory it is a nice idea, but the reality is that these harnesses are heavy and restrict the dog's movement. While wearing one, a dog cannot freely move their shoulders because the harness is wrapped around them. This is not how a harness should be; it should not rub and it should have front and back places to attach the lead. Lastly, I would look for a harness that you do not need to push over your dog's head, as many dogs absolutely hate this feeling and will actively start to run away as soon as they see the harness. So options for a dog to step into and be clipped or buckled up are much better.

A note on lead walking

For me, it is never OK to walk your dog off lead on a pavement, beside a road. It doesn't matter how well behaved you believe them to be, I don't think it is fair or responsible to risk your dog's life. All you need is a dog to be in heat or to see something they have never seen before, and they could bolt in front of a car.

Leads

For me, the right lead for most dogs would be a regular leather, rope or non-stretchy material lead of no more than a metre and a half long for street walking.

I am not a fan of extendable/flexi leads, unless for a very specific reason such as an elderly dog, or a dog that feels safer on a lead but still wants to move around. The issue with flexi leads on the street is that your dog is too far away from you, and you have too little control over it. Your dog may run into the road and you are too far away to stop it. They can also encourage a dog to pull because they learn that if they pull, the lead often lengthens.

It sounds really obvious, but do make sure that the clip

of the lead is not too heavy for your dog. I often see very small dogs attached to big heavy leads that are just too much for them and they may refuse to walk.

Training lines are for use in parks and open spaces only, and would be five to eight metres in length for training recall and boundaries while having some sort of control over the dog. The idea is not that you attach it and still let the dog run off!

Clothing

I have no issue with people using a coat for a dog to keep it warm in cold weather, by which I mean near-freezing. A good coat will be made with natural or breathable materials, it won't have a hood, it doesn't need a fake fur lining, it doesn't restrict the dog's movement, it can repel water, and it should be easily washable. Ideally a coat would not need to be pushed on over a dog's head as most dogs do not enjoy this.

A dog's coat should be practical rather than a fashion statement for the owner. It should allow them to be a dog – to run, play and jump without restriction.

If you have a very thin-skinned breed like a whippet or an Italian greyhound, they are likely to need a coat, while breeds like huskies would never need one.

I suggest a dog is best wearing a coat on the way to the park, and early on the walk, but once its body has warmed up you may want to take the coat off, in the same way you'd remove a sweatshirt when you got warm on a run.

In general, dogs do not love being dressed up. I think a

practical coat is fine, but fancy dress is unnecessary. Your dog may submit to it, and tolerate it, but it's just not something a dog wants to do!

I often see dogs wearing full waterproof coats that cover their entire body, including legs. If you really hate a dirty dog that much, I'd advise not getting a dog who is active and likes water and mud – to constrain a dog into a coat like this on every walk is not fair.

CHAPTER NINETEEN

What Your Dog Wants You to Know about Separation Anxiety

I can hand on my heart say that never before have I seen more dogs suffering with becoming distressed, upset and unable to be separated from their owner.

This type of anxiety is probably in the top three of problems that I receive in my emails every week, and it makes up the bulk of the questions I get asked on social media. People hope that a few words of advice will resolve an issue that requires a far greater understanding, in addition to taking hours and weeks of work.

To some extent, breeders are compounding this problem by putting a positive spin on some distressing behaviour. They will use terms like 'they follow me everywhere', 'they hate to miss out', 'they are like my shadow' – all of these phrases sound cute, sweet and endearing even. Owners often proudly tell me about these descriptions. But any dog that fits this description is going to want to be with you all the time. If a breeder describes their dogs this way, you really want to seek out clarity of what they mean, so you can decide if this is the right kind of dog for you.

The three breeds that I see the most for separation anxiety are the Cockapoo, the Cavapoo and the Miniature Smooth-haired Dachshund. But most can be helped to learn to accept being left alone, and also to enjoy it and to not work themselves into a frenzy that ends up impacting on everyone in the home. It is a great deal of work though.

To be clear, no dog wants to be left alone all the time. They are all pack animals that need company and stimulation. There is, however, a humungous difference between a dog that enjoys family life and likes to partake in it compared to a dog who will not sleep in its bed for fear of you leaving the room, or one who will follow you and watch you in the shower, or who will pant itself senseless because you have popped out to post a letter. These are not endearing traits; they are life-limiting traits that will exhaust you and your highly distressed dog. They will cost you a great deal of money to resolve, if you do ever manage to change them.

I have met people whose entire lives have been put on hold, who haven't eaten at a restaurant together in months because one of them must be with the dog at all times. I'm sure this wasn't what they signed up for when they discussed getting a dog together. Not to mention the levels of stress and anxiety that dog is living through every time their owner[s] move around the house. That certainly is not how you want your dog to live their entire life.

To a dog, separation anxiety feels very real and induces panic. To a human it can feel like their dog is being irrational, but there are also many humans who have very irrational fears that can dictate their life.

The next thing to bear in mind is the role that we as the humans play in creating, fulfilling and encouraging the associated behaviours that can help plant the seeds for separation anxiety to grow. These are usually more applicable to dogs that are not affected by a genetic predisposition for separation anxiety. A few examples:

- getting up to follow a puppy every time they move away from us
- following a puppy because we are toilet-training them
- talking to, looking at, or petting a dog who gets up to follow us
- rewarding this following, e.g. petting the dog waiting for you outside the bathroom
- when your dog moves away to rest and you go to them or you pick them up.

I'm far less worried about dogs who share bedrooms with their owners, or who sleep on the sofa with them. Those are all normal behaviours that owners and dogs would like to share together. This won't determine a correlation between a dog struggling to be separated from an owner or not.

There are many more, but these are the most common and are usually done without thinking, without considering what we are teaching a puppy. If we want our dogs to be independent and carefree when we are not around, we have to select good breeders and we have to then put the groundwork in immediately.

We do also have to remember that other factors can be at play here too:

- genetics
- a rescue dog who was dumped
- an associated experience such as injury or pain
- previous owners who handled things differently
- panic

Due to people being fearful of where a dog may toilet, we can teach a puppy to not be independent within a couple of weeks. Instead, put floor protectors down, take up all your rugs, install baby gates or shut the doors to where you don't want your dog to pee. And then the rest of the time, let them have some freedom, let them explore, let them get away from you and your obsessive eye!

FIRST WE START BY CREATING CONFIDENCE WITHIN THE DOG

Many online tutorials seem to advise telling people to go out of a room for five minutes, then return; then go out for ten minutes; and so on. Unfortunately just closing a door on your dog and hoping for the best is not going to build confidence in an anxious dog or puppy. All this process will do is whip your puppy up into a desperate frenzy of panic and fear, resulting eventually in barking, yipping, panting and crying. You certainly won't make it to thirty minutes and by the time you have reached fifteen minutes you will be wanting to pull your own hair out. So just stop. Don't bother trying to utilise that system. It is old, outdated and based on distress, not confidence building.

The system we are going to use is to teach a puppy to

relax in our presence, to not worry about us, that they don't need to sleep with one eye open for fear of us disappearing. Because we aren't going anywhere, yet.

We do also have to go at the pace of our dog, as every dog is different, and so is their genetic make-up, their background, the socialisation and so forth. But these are the basic principles to build up confidence in a puppy or dog with separation anxiety.

At first, stick around while they are sleeping.

We must not creep out or away when a puppy is sleeping. If they wake up and you are gone, the panic will start and they will come to find you. It should be no big deal; you're not touching them or sticking close, you're just around in the same room, doing your thing.

Begin to disconnect before they go to sleep

We should start to remove ourselves from being available before a puppy drops off to sleep. For instance, we remain in the same room but perhaps we are on the sofa while they are in their bed, so there is distance and disconnection but the puppy is not being left alone. We still want our dogs to feel comforted and supported.

Use chews strategically

Only provide chews when you are going to be around, not as a way of distracting your dog so you can exit. Otherwise the chew will then become a trigger that you are going to abandon them and they will stop using it.

Instead, give them a chew that they can work on, while you are in the room but not while they are touching you, sitting on you or lying on you. The chew should indicate that they can relax and you will be around.

Puppy-proof your home to build independence

If your home is puppy-proofed, when they do get up to explore, you don't need to follow them for fear of them eating an electric cable or cracking open the hair gel that you left under your bed in your washbag.

Don't make a big deal of their every appearance

When your dog rejoins you from a little exploration trip around the house, do not look up, and don't talk to them as they walk back in. I don't praise my husband every time he enters the room! He probably wishes I would.

Independence is more important than toilet accidents

If they have had a wee on their exploration, just go and clear it up a short while later, don't make a big deal of it. Accidents will happen, but learning independence is far more important than a wee on the floor once in a while.

Don't let them become distressed

Do not abandon your puppy/dog, make them cry it out or leave them to become distressed. In the early days, when you are working on separation anxiety, work out a schedule so that someone can be around. Factor in months to work on this, not weeks. And if you cannot be around, then you need to factor in a trusted person with whom your dog can also build a bond but who will follow all that you are doing to the letter – consistency is essential.

Don't try to rush it

I know it is tempting to try and get the dog to be left alone, but if you try to whizz through things, it will come back to bite you. I tell any client approaching me to factor in six months, sometimes longer, to get a puppy or dog to the happy point of being able to not see you and to be on their own.

One size doesn't fit all

I don't do a one size fits all, as perhaps you are reading this with a rescue dog who was dropped off at a rescue centre and then rehomed to you. If that dog has experienced an owner taking them somewhere and then never returning, it has a good reason to panic when you attempt to walk out of the room. The steps we put in place might be different from that of a puppy who has been well bred and isn't starting off with any issues to begin with. I am sure you can see the difference. Work with a trusted behaviourist if you are dealing with a complicated separation issue.

A DOG ISN'T DESTRUCTIVE ON PURPOSE

Sometimes people will believe that they have succeeded in getting their dog to spend time alone, only to realise that they are in fact being destructive when left alone. Owners often tell me that a dog in this situation 'knows it's done a bad thing'.

This actually isn't factually true. What the dog learns is that you enter a room, go over to the item they chewed and you shout and/or reprimand them and they will anticipate this with fear. But they will also feel relieved, as the chewing of the item appeared to bring you back into the room, as it was the first thing you touched and paid attention to when you re-entered the room. So you can see from a dog's point of view why they may chew again, and why our behaviour may unwittingly fuel that particular fire.

If your dog is being destructive when left, you will need to film them, to record their behaviour to pinpoint exactly when they begin to feel anxious or distressed. Destruction is not carried out simply because a dog wants to annoy you – it will be done either out of boredom or usually because it is so panicked, it simply must try to regulate its own emotions by grinding, biting down on or pulling something up, e.g. a carpet. All of these behaviours will help a dog calm themselves, but they also may pant through stress and find it very hard to calm down even when you return. These outlets are also indicative of a dog in a panicked emotional state. When we are in this kind of mode, we aren't thinking, we lash out, we grab, we try anything, and the same is true of a dog in this state.

If you notice your dog is showing signs of destruction, don't wait for it to escalate, or become so bad that you feel your only option is to rehome the dog.

I would advise working with a trusted behaviourist from the start, so problems don't arise later.

CHAPTER TWENTY

What Your Dog Wants You to Know about Feeling Safe

Every dog needs a safe space, and it is your job as the owner to provide it. By a safe space I mean somewhere the dog can go where it knows it will be left alone and given space. This can be its bed or a crate. Children should understand that they must always leave a dog alone when it is in its safe space – if they are too young to understand, then it will be up to you to ensure the dog is not bothered by them.

A dog needs a safe place[s] to retreat, to seek solace and to relax, in order to reduce the risk of aggression as a reaction to being pushed, overpetted, when it's too noisy, etc. By a safe space, I don't just mean a bed. I'd suggest you should also seek to create a room that they feel comfortable going in without you. For example, I use my bedroom for Pip if we have lots of kids in the house and I feel that he needs space. He will actively take himself off there too.

Many puppies will squeeze themselves into very random gaps, under sofas, under a coffee table, in the nook at the back of the room behind some boxes. As an owner, it is often tempting to move them somewhere 'comfier', which usually means somewhere that we have created and seems ideal to us. But the puppy has chosen its own refuge because it feels secure, and we must respect that choice and allow them to rest where they feel best.

Seeking refuge is something all animals need to do. We as humans do the same but without even realising it. We may not choose to walk on busy paths, or we may choose to avoid a coffee shop we don't like for a particular reason. The same applies to puppies and dogs. And those boundaries and refuge-seeking instincts need to be respected.

I'd even go as far as to say that dogs need a couple of areas to be able to retreat to, depending on what is going on and the make-up of your household and set-up of your home. To use my own example, Pip has a bed in our downstairs living area, tucked into an alcove where he can also see all that is happening. He also has a bed upstairs in our bedroom, tucked in by my wardrobe and the radiator.

The bed upstairs and the one downstairs allow him to move around depending on the noise levels of my children, how tired he is, how much he wants to be involved versus how much he wants to sleep. The activity levels of our rescue kittens can also impact where he likes to rest, as the kittens sometimes like to try to play with his tail! If, for example, he is really worn out from a previous day's activities I will know, as he won't get out of his bed upstairs and will want to just rest there most of the morning, which is fine.

The position of your beds or refuge areas are important

to observe, as some you may create yourself and some your dog make create on their own. My deaf Bulldog, Cookie, used to go around to my side of the bed and lie there, tucked away, as it made her feel safe and protected and happy. She would prefer to lie on the floorboards, as they were draughty, and she liked that. She could also feel us approaching, as she was deaf, so in an old Victorian flat the original boards would move when we walked on them, alerting her that someone was there as she couldn't hear us.

Underneath a sofa or coffee table can be a brilliant retreat, as only a dog can get under there, so they can lie down and watch at a distance. I often go to clients' homes and they go to pull the dog out from a safe space, or try to use treats to lure them out. If you can, I'd leave them to figure that out themselves. And I certainly wouldn't be allowing children to interfere, pull, lure or drag a dog out of a space.

Many rescue dogs may need much more time to adapt and be left alone where they choose to rest and sleep. A scared, nervous puppy may do the same. Blocking up where they want to retreat to will not make them feel happier or more trusting of you. It merely removes their place to calm down and figure things out. The only reason I'd block off a place where a dog has sought refuge would be if it were unsafe – for example, lying on top of the TV cables.

A retreat should allow a dog to catch their breath, for their heartbeat to return to normal, to not feel threatened and relaxed enough to switch off and sleep.

CHAPTER TWENTY-ONE

What Your Dog Wants You to Know
about Behavioural Issues

By the time clients contact me about behavioural issues, they have usually had a problem with their dog's behaviour for at least six months. That is six months in which the problem behaviour has been reinforced and continued, and it means that it is going to take a while to undo. So the most important thing your dog wants you to know is that its behaviour is trying to tell you something NOW. Even if it's inconvenient or embarrassing or it feels like something the dog might grow out of, the sooner you address what your dog is trying to tell you, the sooner the issue will be resolved. Please don't wait until a problem is severe before contacting an expert.

No healthy, well-bred dog is born with an unmanageable behavioural issue. These problems begin because we as humans create these issues and that is done in one of two ways:

1. We buy a dog that has been so poorly bred, raised and

socialised that a problem is fundamentally built into the hardwiring and genetics of the dog.

2. We either ignore or react in such a way to a dog's behaviour over days, weeks and months that the behaviour then becomes either a habit for the dog or simply a default way of responding because they feel that they have no other options.

I will always remember the elderly bull-breed boy sitting in the rehoming-centre kennels, pining his heart out for his family. He was put into the rescue because for ten years of his life his family had encouraged him to bark at the door to alert them when someone was approaching. Then after a decade of rewarding him for this behaviour, they had a baby. Suddenly the dog's barking at the door became a problem, as it woke the baby. Yet they were the very people who taught and encouraged their puppy to start this behaviour, getting him excited by running to the door whenever there was a noise, then petting and stroking him as he started to make some grumbles, and being pleased when this turned to barking, so that they knew someone was approaching the house. How on earth could this boy know that the people he trusted, that he was trying to respond to, would actually throw him out, discard him because his behaviour no longer suited their lifestyle? It broke my heart to see him sitting wondering where his gang had gone.

It is these kinds of experiences that have stuck with me for ever. You never stop thinking about those dogs whose heart broke through no fault of their own. I saw countless dogs in London council pound kennels, where the dog warden gets called out or has to collect a dog that has been discarded. Some of the stories I could relay to you would make you sob, but really the main message to get across is that as the human in the relationship, you are the one who is empowered to make the right decisions about problem behaviours. You have to use this decision-making process very carefully and even if you do make mistakes, as we all do, it is how you deal with them and work to amend things that matters the most.

Prevention is always better than looking for a cure, but issues do arise and it is better to deal with them early so that they do not get any worse.

RESOURCE GUARDING

This is when a dog defends an item or an object. It could be food-related or it could be something very random. I've known of a dog who fiercely defended the fluff that came off a carpet, so the defending isn't usually about the actual object, it is more about what we have taught them we will do about it.

Consider the process of having a young eight-week-old puppy who, after settling in, begins to explore the house or flat. When they happen upon something of interest, it will be sniffed and will often go straight into their mouth. This is actually for sensory feedback reasons, to feel the object, to explore it and most often it will then be discarded and dropped. Usually, though, the dog doesn't get this chance to explore because the overzealous pup owner is already clawing the object out of their mouth. So the dog allows this and moves on, to carry on exploring their environment. They come across another unfamiliar object. Once again, the exact same process happens. It goes in the mouth and then gets clawed out by human fingers.

Later that afternoon, the same puppy gets let out into the garden, exploring a new space, picking up items as it goes to understand what it is and each time their jaw is prised open and the item released. By the end of that day, the puppy has learned a really important lesson, that when an item is of interest, the human wants it more than them and that the human will challenge them to get hold of it.

Now imagine if you have a dog who has been raised in a large litter, has been fed from a single bowl among its eight other littermates and had to compete for food from day dot. The slightest challenge over a resource is going to ignite the fire of challenge. Within days of taking that puppy home, possessive tendencies will start to be displayed and the dog will resist having objects taken away from it, or it may start running off with the item to get far away from you.

If your puppy hasn't been bred in the way I've just described, as in not in a competitive environment, with a large litter, then you stand a chance of preventing resource-guarding tendencies. When you visit a breeder, you are also looking to make sure there are heaps of toys, too many for the puppies to play with, so that competing for resources isn't something that they need to spend their time doing in the imprinting and primary socialisation phase.

The process of pulling the item out of the mouth is often incredibly intrusive, grabbing the dog's head, holding the jaw and shoving fingers down their throat. An experience that they will never have been subjected to before, as dogs do not do this action to each other! Also, with a breeder, they will have been living in a part of the house that is puppy-proofed, so that the only items left on the floor are objects particularly designated as being safe for a puppy to explore and fiddle around with. The exact opposite of the kind of puppy-proofing that many owners do: we expect them to just accept and learn about the many intricacies of our living environments. One household I visited were getting incredibly annoyed with a puppy as it kept brushing up against a vase that they had in the hallway. The vase was worth £50,000. No puppy could ever know that and, even if they did, they still wouldn't care. So if you don't want them near it, on it, touching it, exploring it, then you remove it.

PREVENTING RESOURCE GUARDING

With a puppy or a new rescue dog, I suggest you should actively seek out random, interesting household objects that you just don't care about, that won't cause any harm to a puppy but that you do not need to rush over and 'save them from'. This is really, really important, as it offers opportunities for your puppy or dog to actively learn from.

Everything else that you do care about needs to be got rid of, boxed up and put away until your puppy or dog has grown out of this particular exploratory phase. Remove the kids' Lego, the shoes, the compost bin in easy reach, the plants you don't want them to touch, etc. Life will feel so much more relaxing.

Every day you will place new, safe objects and surfaces out on the floor for your dog or puppy to encounter and engage with. The kinds of objects or items I'd be laying down and supplying should be varied and change constantly. Here are some ideas to get you started:

- cardboard boxes of varying sizes
- screwed-up bits of paper – newspaper, writing paper, envelopes from the post as they will carry their own scent that we can't even determine
- bits of hosepipe
- hessian bags for life
- large Tupperware containers
- rinsed-out coffee takeaway cups with no lid
- metal tablespoon
- rubber ladle or spatula
- old magazines
- books you aren't too bothered about
- tea towel
- large scraps of cotton fabric that are heavyweight
- old towel
- random items of clothes belonging to other people (if I ever buy second-hand/vintage bits, before I wash them, I lay them on the floor and let the animals explore them as there will be heaps of scent we don't know about)
- thick rolls of masking tape
- used egg boxes
- enamel camping cups and plates
- corkboard tiles

- fabric dishcloths that you are planning to throw out
- pad of Post-it notes
- balls of ribbon
- cricket pads
- deflated football (don't kick it around, just have it for them to meet, see, learn about).

I could go on and on with this list, but I think this gives you enough of a picture.

The idea isn't that they should actively be picking these up to chew on, but they are things that, if they did, you don't need to rush to take them away from them. We don't engage or play with these items. We just allow them to be available. So a puppy or dog has the time to sniff them, to lick them, to perhaps try wrapping their teeth around them, but we can carry on doing what we are doing and not rush over and grab them.

In addition to this, within the mix of household items I'd also put some more edible things – again, things that you can leave down and not worry about. But so the mix on the floor varies every day, include foods such as:

- Carrots
- Pumpkin
- Baby tomatoes
- Slices of apple
- Green leaves (e.g. cabbage, kale, spinach)
- Green beans
- Blueberries
- Cucumber.

We need to be actively supplying exploration activities, and sensory sensations that can be mouthed and then discarded. So that if they pick the item up and walk off with it, you just leave them be. This kind of activity needs to be done every single day, chopping and changing the items you are putting down. We need to make the exploration an acceptable behaviour that they will grow out of in a few weeks if you handle it properly. The only caveat to this is if there are also nutritional issues at play. Scavenging can be driven by hormone imbalances or from a poor, dry diet.

On top of this, if they do pick up something that they decide to sit down with and give it a gnaw, I'd like you to become involved in the exploration. Not to remove it but to show them you actively won't be taking it away, so we avoid the idea of the stealing of things and running off with it becoming a chase game.

You could even sit on the floor among the items as they explore, and let them do their own thing. If they pick something up and look as pleased as punch with themselves, then you give them a little clap, praise them and just stroke their body, so that you encourage them to not see you as a grabbing threat, and that you do not touch the actual object, only the dog.

What you should start to see is that within a few days, if they start to pick up a particular object, they will begin to pick it up and bring it onto your lap or lay right next to you, so you can just sit and stroke them. Keep it calm and relaxed, non-threatening and non-challenging.

This process is about showing your dog that there is no competition for items, and they do not need to feel scared that you will rip things from them. I usually encourage my clients to put a phrase or command to the picking up of items. I use 'what have you got?' as you naturally want to say this in a questioning tone, where your voice goes up at the end, so it instantly sounds happier and non-threatening. When they come over, waggling, to show you, you simply continue petting them, not touching the item. Should you want them to actually drop it, to not chew on it, you can then walk away from them and make it sound like what you are doing is far more interesting – e.g. walk out into another room and rustle around, or bang a cupboard door, so they instinctively want to come and explore what is going on, usually dropping the item and following. You can then provide them with a more interesting item to pop in their mouth that you are happier with and that poses no threat, e.g. a chew that they can actually eat. And someone else can discard the item you didn't want them eating. But do this when they have left the room, so it isn't confrontational. We are trying to prevent a life of competing over objects, scraps, food and toys.

Many people question this method, worrying that they will end up a dog who picks things up and brings them to you, thinking that they may be rewarded for it. And my simple answer is yes, you may well create a dog that does this. And I'd much rather live with a dog who believes that sharing receives rewards than a dog who will defend an item, who would bite my children in order to retain an item, and who will snarl and growl out of fear of something being ripped away from them.

EATING THEIR OWN POO,
OR ANOTHER ANIMAL'S POO

This is so grim and, not surprisingly, owners are always horrified by this behaviour. As far as a dog is concerned, though, poo is just another resource; it is just something that they produced. The two main reasons for a dog eating their own poo are:

1. To hide it, due to being reprimanded for toileting accidents when younger.
2. Due to a lack of nutrients, minerals and proof that the food they are being fed is not meeting their nutritional needs. For example, I've never come across a dog who does this that is fed raw food or a fresh diet. In my experience, it's always dogs fed on a dry kibble diet.

Reason number two can also be true of dogs who are eating cat poo, fox poo, etc. Depending on the animal's faeces that they are seeking out or consuming, it can be an indicator of the nutrients that are missing, and a great nutritionist will be able to figure this out for you. For example, the contents of cat poo are very different from that of horse or cow poo.

Our Great Dane, Fred, arrived from the rescue on the thin side. It was really difficult to keep any weight on him and I used to watch him hoovering up cat poo in our garden from our cat, Lemon. It took a number of months to get Fred's supplementation just right, but one of the ways I knew it was working was when he could go into the garden and not give the poo a second glance!

Poo eating certainly isn't something you have to just live with or accept. It isn't something you should reprimand, as grim as it is, because it is driven by a psychological need or deficiency, and it isn't something that they are choosing to do.

Do be very careful if your dog is consuming human faeces, as very often this can make a dog extremely ill and sometimes they may require hospitalisation. Human poo that a dog finds in a park may contain drugs or alcohol, so if you ever suspect this has happened, do seek veterinary advice immediately. If your dog is partial to poo eating or you live in an area where it is very difficult to avoid, then you should seriously consider muzzling your dog so that it cannot keep happening. I would prefer a few months' worth of muzzling while you get on top of the issue rather than risking the dog's life by letting it happen while the dog cannot physically control themselves.

OBSESSIVE BEHAVIOURS — TRYING TO AVOID OCD IN YOUR DOG

There are some breeds that are bred to not have an off switch, to just keep working, to keep going, to work harder and faster. This can be OK if you are also working that dog for the purpose it was designed for, e.g. herding, searching an airport or working out in a field for hours on end. The problems arise when a family or household purchase a dog of this kind, thinking that they are 'active' so that will suffice. There really is a large gaping rift between liking to go for a run at the weekend and a dog working for twelve-hour shifts at an airport, sniffing out illegal substances.

Often we take these types of dogs who are high drive, high energy and then have to find ways to channel their energy. So the 'easiest' option is to pick up a ball lobber and a ball of some kind. It starts with a few throws and a puppy subsequently being tired and sleeping, which means it's more pleasant for an owner of one of these kinds of dogs. However, by starting this kind of exercise regime young, what we actually end up doing is training a kind of supercharged athlete who just gets fitter and fitter and fitter until we can no longer wear them out; no physical output tires them – nothing touches the side. And we have also created an obsession with an item or object as the dog has been taught this from a young age.

The other reason this kind of obsession can begin is where you have an anxious or worried dog, who doesn't feel confident. The dog doesn't want to interact in the park; it doesn't like the external environment, stimulus and people and dogs. So an owner starts trying to utilise something to bring the dog out of its shell, or to give it something else to focus on. The ball is often produced and by playing these types of games we increase adrenaline, the heart rate is raised and it looks like the dog is having a whale of a time.

The issue is more that we don't ever really address the anxiety or worry that the dog has. So the ball also starts to be linked as a general coping strategy for times of stress and slowly creeps into every aspect of everyday life.

A very easy way to test if your dog has an obsessive behaviour, e.g. with a tennis ball, is to see:

- Does your dog not want to interact with any other dogs/people?
- Can your dog eat or drink when the ball is out?
- Is your dog able to accept a treat when the ball is around?
- Is your dog able to follow another cue that you are certain s/he knows?
- When you put the ball away, how long is their recovery period, as in how long does it take them to either switch off or to relax?
- Are they willing to play with the ball until they are at the point of exhaustion?
- If you were to put the ball in a cupboard, or behind a fence, how long would the dog spend trying to get to the item? Would they start whining, crying or digging?
- Is your dog fixated on your hand/bag where the ball resides?

There is a very distinct difference between a dog that enjoys playing ball and is active in the game, and a dog that is obsessed.

What is important if you have a dog that is on the nervous, fearful or anxious side is that you don't brush this obsessive behaviour under the carpet. While the ball can still have a role in their life, you wouldn't want it to become their sole reason for being. Although it may feel like you are solving one problem, you actually aren't – all that happens is that the fear and anxiety will actually just now revolve around that ball.

There are many other factors to place importance on when broadening your dog's horizons, such as mental stimulation, training games, sniffing games, environmental enrichment and general sensory regulation. Try not to be reliant on one format, one toy or one type of game. It doesn't have to be a million and one different things; it is just about knowing your dog in more depth to carve out the right way for them.

DOWN, DOG, DOWN – HOW TO NOT ENCOURAGE A DOG TO JUMP UP

I do find that there are certain breeds, like the Hungarian Vizsla, the Whippet, the German Short-haired Pointer and the Pomeranian, who love to dance around on their back legs more than many other dogs do.

So, for those dogs that love to do a two-legged parade, you could definitely think about putting this dance to a cue word.

If, however, you would like to understand the behaviour a bit more, you need to look at what your dog may be getting out of jumping up. Usually when a dog jumps up it is because we have inadvertently taught them that all the good things come from above, e.g. treats, the food bowl, chews, the lead, etc.

Many dogs will start to jump up to bridge the gap between themselves and the reward, or to speed up the rate at which you provide the reward. Some will jump up as it gets you to push them down, which although it is negative, it is still physical contact that they weren't receiving previously. Lastly, children often encourage or teach a dog to jump up, usually with the type of toy playing they do. Children tend to hold toys and dangle them, so that when the dog walks towards them the child will pull the toy up, often out of fear of being mouthed on. The dog very quickly learns to anticipate this type of game, and will run and jump or lunge for the toy.

If we look at the ways we interact and the things we focus on and encourage, you can usually find small ways to reinforce the behaviours you like – e.g. a dog who chooses to sit as a way of saying 'please' is far more favourable than a dog who jumps up for everything.

In order to teach this, we do have to look at allowing the dog to make some decisions of their own that we either walk away from or we reinforce.

With children, all games should happen on the floor, all toys should be on the floor, and all balls should be rolled, not thrown overarm, as otherwise, if played in the opposite way, the dog can very easily and quickly learn to jump and you will then spend your life trying to reverse what your children taught it so quickly! Believe me, I know. My daughter taught our Great Dane to rest his head on our kitchen table within a couple of days. She taught it by drip-feeding him the scrambled egg she didn't want, slowly sliding it across the table off her plate and straight into his big old slobbery jowls. He thought it was marvellous and so did she.

A GREAT WAY TO TEACH A
NO-JUMPING-UP POLICY DURING PLAY

- Make sure your dog is in the right frame of mind to play: not manic, not overtired, not too energetic, or else you will find this incredibly hard to teach. Timing is everything, especially with a young dog.
- Use a toy that your dog enjoys playing with but that won't make them too excited, crazed or out of control – preferably something that you can hold on to, like a tugger toy, rather than a ball.
- Play with the toy on the floor, allowing your dog to pick it up and play with it, tug on it, and so on.
- After a couple of repetitions, hold the toy in your hands so they cannot access it and wait for the dog to stop trying to get hold of it and to either choose to step back or put their bottom on the floor. Then release the toy on the floor. The key is that you don't ask them to do anything, but let them figure out what you are looking for from them, otherwise it defeats the purpose of the game.
- Once they can do the previous step every single time, with no hesitation, you do the same thing, but when the toy is covered in your hands and they have stepped back or sat (of their own choosing), do a slight hand raise with the toy, just a couple of centimetres off the floor, and then bring the toy straight back down to the ground and let the dog take the toy.
- The idea is to slowly introduce the dog to the movement

of the toy, but with the toy only being played with when it returns to the floor.

- Again, when they can do the tiny step of watching the toy in your hands being raised and hold their position (without being told), then you can slowly take it up a couple more centimetres and repeat.
- You must not rush the process, and you must not try to skip ahead and start waving the toy around and expect the dog to not jump up for it.
- Know that certain breeds may take longer or find this harder. A terrier who is movement-motivated will need much longer to become accustomed to the game, in comparison to a Cavalier King Charles Spaniel.
- When you also look at the list above about how to introduce a level of control around a dog jumping for a toy, you can start to see why so many end up doing the opposite. As most people don't teach it like this, we just expect them to inherently know not to jump for things, which is a bonkers thought – we expect manners we haven't yet taught.

You will also need to pay attention to any times when you are actively encouraging the jumping up. For example, when you come in from work, are you happy to see your dog and so don't mind them jumping up at you? But when you are getting ready to leave for work, you don't want them jumping up? Your dog won't be able to determine the difference.

Instead of ignoring your dog when you come in (as many will advise and something I'm not keen on), you can teach your dog that when you return from work it is still fun, it is still playtime, but use a toy that your dog either has to carry or that is long and attached to a rope. You can walk in and hold it so that the toy touches the ground while you stand, and the dog can tug and pull and play, all with four feet on the ground.

Lastly, when you are rewarding with treats, try to offer them to your dog from underneath their jaw, to completely get rid of the belief that all treats come from above. If you imagine your dog has gone into the 'sit' position, instead of giving a treat as they look up at you, lower a cupped hand so that their head points towards the floor, and then reward from the hand. So that actually your dog may learn to look up at its owner but doesn't expect the treat to be given from above.

I do the same thing by also dropping treats onto the floor. This can be especially good for larger-breed dogs, as people are definitely not going to feel comfortable if they launched themselves at them. Again, if your dog is taught that treats come from below, this will always be beneficial to reduce jumping-up behaviour.

One thing I would reiterate is that sometimes the jumping-up behaviour can also be a way of expressing anxiety. If you tend to find that the jumping up at your legs and sometimes even jumping up and grabbing clothes happens when you are outside, in the park, in more social situations, do try to take a step back and assess the reasons behind it. For example, some dogs may start this kind of behaviour when on busy roads, where there is more noise than they feel comfortable with. Some dogs may start doing it around groups of other dogs, or dogs that make them feel uncomfortable or intimidated. So do listen. Do get your dog out, do remove them and don't make them stick it out.

The jumping about is being used as they know that you will respond, that you will do something, so it becomes a way of activating you. Although it isn't ideal, it is better that your dog tells you in this way than by being aggressive to the dog[s] involved. However, if you don't take note and you don't adapt the ways you are doing things, this angst will only progress and possibly start to develop into more reactive behaviour. The same can be true of dogs who are jumping up at the lead and grabbing it, tugging it and then holding in their mouth to try to ignite a game. Take notice of when this happens.

AGGRESSION WITH OTHER DOGS

It is worth saying that aggression really deserves an entire book of its own, but I do feel it needs a brief overview. I have already covered body language with other dogs in Chapter Fifteen, and if you pay close attention to your dog and to the dogs around it, you can hopefully avoid situations of aggression before they begin. However, you may have a dog who sometimes uses aggression as a response, and it's worth bearing a few things in mind.

A reactive dog (one who reacts when they see triggering stimulus) can be created through many pathways. Breeding is an easy one to understand, in that a dog was bred from an aggressive bitch and in turn has produced a litter with aggressive tendencies. Do bear in mind that some of these traits are not always actually aggressive, e.g. a Jack Russell that has been bred on a farm to be feisty for a job may not then make an ideal family pet. That doesn't mean it is an aggressive dog, it means that we have taken a dog designed and bred for a different purpose and we have tried to turn them into something they are not. We do always need to bear this in mind. Are we simply trying to fit a square peg into a round hole?

With other types of aggression towards dogs, the most common routes are:

Frustration that turns to aggression

A puppy that is taught to go up to every dog they see and interact with them. Then, as they get older, owners try to keep them apart, so the dog starts to get frustrated on the lead, pulling, lunging, crying and whining. Eventually, for many dogs, this frustration builds over a period of time and we end up with lead-aggressive dogs. These are dogs who see another dog while on a lead and go into reaction mode, by using aggression like lunging, barking and growling as their frustration has reached a point where it has tipped over and is now a full-on reaction each time they see a dog.

Intimidation turned reactive

This is where the puppy who was worried around other dogs, who often felt intimidated, gets taught to get rid of the dogs themselves, as no one else is going to do it for them. Green-light signals get missed early on, so dogs run over and bombard and overwhelm the puppy. This kind of feeling won't be tolerated for ever if we don't step in to assist and remove the puppy.

Poor breeding and socialisation

This is an easy part to correct, by not buying or selecting a breeder that is creating dogs who at eight weeks are already entering the world in a fearful, worried and anxious state. If you visit a breeder and the dog[s] are showing signs you feel concerned about, walk away, as the amount of appalling breeders I've seen and heard make excuses for the fear-aggressive dogs they have created is a list I could fill this book with. These bad breeders have also meant I've had clients who have had to have their four-, five- or six-month-old puppies put to sleep.

There are of course many other ways that aggression towards other dogs can begin and be shaped. This isn't supposed to be exhaustive, but to highlight three ways that are common and that you as an owner can take control of and prevent are by the way you select, the way you social-ise and the way you teach your dog to interact with other dogs. It should feel like you now know how to prevent it in some cases.

PREVENTING AGGRESSION TOWARDS PEOPLE — PAINTING A PICTURE OF HOW IT CAN BEGIN

A few days ago, I visited the home of a ten-month-old dog who spent nearing two hours barking at me, from upstairs, from behind a door, from in a utility room, from on a lead. The owners tried lots of things to see if he could acclimatise to me being present. He actually couldn't calm down, he didn't calm down, and the mere presence of me sent him into an immediate frenzied panic that meant he was not capable of reacting in any other way, except to make sure I did not come anywhere near him or approach him. His aggression was making it very clear that he did not welcome guests, and that he perceived them as an issue. He certainly did not want any kind of contact. I couldn't even look at him.

This kind of fear in adolescent and adult dogs is actually really common and is very different from a dog who just isn't drawn to strangers or people they don't know. There are lots of dogs who like to keep themselves to themselves, prefer to keep their gang small and don't need to say hi to everyone. That is fine.

Aggression and reactive behaviour to humans is rather different, as it poses a threat either in public or in the home and both can be dangerous to passers-by, visitors or households and should be taken very seriously. According to the law, a homeowner can be held accountable for their dog's actions in the home so, at the very least, you would need to have a degree of safety management in place so that if your dog is showing signs of reactivity, they cannot get to people and they cannot bite. In my opinion, this is your legal obligation.

Once again, this is too much of a broad subject to delve into – an entire book could be written on it – but it is important to understand how to prevent this happening to your puppy. It will greatly depend on the puppy-rearing your individual dog has experienced. For example, a rescue puppy I met, who had witnessed his siblings being beaten to death by various humans and his mother also dying at the hands of humans, may never, ever recover from this experience. His real-life experience is too great to overcome without the assistance of medication and even then the trauma may be too great to achieve what the owners desire, which is to have a dog who is excited to see all humans. We often need to adapt our expectations and goals.

For most dogs, the fear is usually due to a lack of decent breeding, a lack of calm, considerate handling, and a breed's noise sensitivity can also contribute. And then obviously there is the implication of the secondary social-isation period when you bring your puppy home at eight weeks old.

Let's look at how, for some puppies, the fear of humans may begin at eight to twelve weeks.

You have brought your eight-week-old puppy home and are super-excited to have people come over to meet your dog, because they all want to see and play with your new addition. So your first family members come over and it usually happens in one of four ways:

1. The family come in and sit down and you pick up the puppy and simply put him on the family member's lap, because of course he's going to want to go right up to them, isn't he?
2. You leave the puppy on the floor, family enter the room and as he lies in his bed or sits on the floor, the family members go right over to him, picking him up and petting him.
3. The puppy is on the floor sitting by your feet. As new people come in, he seeks some refuge to watch and assess the situation, perhaps behind your legs. As your guests arrive, you want them all to see him, so you move your legs from in front of him, so he is no longer shielded. And then a family member swoops by and picks him up, or you pass him straight over.
4. He's been in someone's lap and gets bitey, so they pop him down and he shakes it off and goes and sits elsewhere to recover. Another person then goes to sit next to him, or sits close and pops them on their lap on the floor.

All four scenarios may result in the same outcome: a fearful interaction with people coming into the dog's space in the home environment, their apparent safe space. And this experience will only build as you have more and more people coming over to see you and the puppy.

The main issue is that we give the puppy no time to assess, to figure out what's going on and to be able to approach in their own time, because we as humans want that puppy cuddle, we want the contact, even if the dog doesn't want it.

It will only take a couple more repetitions of this scenario

THE BOOK YOUR DOG WISHES YOU WOULD READ

to build up a picture for your dog: that humans are to be feared. Especially those entering the home, as they will not take your cues of distancing yourself, they won't let you remove yourself, and they won't allow you to watch from a distance and then interact when you feel ready.

It's rather like you sitting at home, minding your own business, when a group of people arrive that you don't know and you are supposed to turn into the life and soul of the party, immediately. It is sort of bonkers that we place that level of expectation on a baby animal when you look at it that way.

This same scenario is true of dogs out and about in public, when they are walking along streets, getting to know the world. They are starting to fathom out what the big world holds, when people start swooping into their life, trying to pet them, to grab them, to touch them, which can feel overbearing. I've had clients who have been out with their puppy on a lead and a total stranger has come from behind and picked their puppy up, without asking and without any kind of permission, which is obviously incredibly scary for both the dog and its owner.

During a puppy's fear period, events like this can potentially add to the problem. If your puppy was pretty confident and then there are a few incidents during a tricky time, you may find the knock-on impact pretty big. Try to look at the cues that your dog is showing you:

- A dog who is unsure and needs more space
- Doesn't go seeking people out, but happily stays close on or off lead

- If they do go up to investigate, they are very hesitant and don't want to be petted; they just want to sniff to suss things out
- May start scrabbling at your legs to get lifted out
- May start barking to get you to do something or move on
- Their head bobs down if someone goes to pet them
- Feels frantic around people and pulls to get to somewhere calmer
- Needs time to sit and watch and listen and learn.

I have often found that smaller dogs can really develop this issue due to the amount of times owners, visitors and random strangers on the street pick up the dog without giving the dog a chance to refuse the pick-up. I do feel that we should be operating on the basis of seeing if being handled is something the dog itself wants.

But how do you ask a dog if it wants to be picked up?

I would advise kneeling down and seeing if the dog climbs onto your lap and into your arms. If it does so, then it wouldn't mind being picked up and held. If it doesn't, then it's unlikely to want that kind of physical contact. If the dog is scrabbling at your legs to be picked up, that is also an easy cue to read and react to. To check if they enjoy being in a bag, you can pop the bag on the ground to see if they hop in.

If the puppy sits next to your legs or leans, that still doesn't warrant being picked up. The contact can be a safety lean – many big dogs do this too – but it doesn't mean you should try to lift up your Doberman onto your lap!

I always think you should imagine that little puppy as a fully grown Rottweiler or Mastiff. Would you still be doing that action with that dog? If the answer is no, then you should probably leave the dog alone!

HOW TO MOVE ON FROM AN AWFUL DOG WALK WITH YOUR PUPPY OR DOG

We've all had those walks where something difficult has happened. This is part of dog ownership: some days the dog walk is all split poo bags and not listening and a disagreement with another dog owner, and others it's sunshine and rainbows.

- Remember that walks are a roller coaster – some days are good and some are bad. Even if you have ended up arguing with those you are walking with, you can still learn from it. I often have these kinds of walks when my children are towing along!
- Look at where the issues came from – was it too distracting, were there too many dogs, was it too noisy? Whatever it is that you can identify, you need to change it on the next walk.
- Don't run before you can walk. It is easy to say but harder to remember. It is true, though. With a puppy, you must take it very, very slowly. With a rescue dog, you must too. Gently and quietly is always better.
- Did you put too much pressure on yourself? Were you trying to cram lots into a day? Were you with the kids? Did you bump into a friend and end up getting

distracted? All of these things happen. It's what we do with the learnings that matters.

- Tiny details can affect the nature of the walk. For some dogs, a certain surface can send them into a tizzy. For others, bike riders cycling everywhere can prove to be an overload. It is all about knowing what works for you and your dog and your family.
- Alternate where you walk. Try not to always walk in the place that is closest to your house. Variety is important but so is a combination of quiet and busier places. If you only walk your dog down a busy high street, you may find it hard to ever have a great walk, if the noise jars your dog and sets the tone for a bad walk.
- Make sure you factor in time to walk alone with your dog – purely so you can see if you being distracted, with the kids or on your phone, is also impacting the dog walk.
- Try not to hold a grudge! Easier said than done, but cut your dog some slack and move forward for the next walk. Holding a grudge against your dog can end up creating a vicious cycle of behaviour because you keep believing they will behave in this way, but change will only happen if you do things differently.
- Seek help. If it really does feel like Groundhog Day every time you walk the dog, then seek help from a behaviourist you trust and like. Working on it early will mean there is far less work to do, rather than just leaving it and hoping it will change. If you do have a disappointing walk, make the next one super-simple,

super-quiet, super-sniffy and where no one else goes. Everyone needs a breather sometimes.

WHY IT'S OK TO CAVE IN AND OTHER TIPS AND PHRASES YOU MAY HEAR BUT SHOULD IGNORE:

- 'Caving in' is often a phrase used by people to tell you that you should not 'cave in' to your dog's whining, their crying, their pleas. I'd actually say the exact opposite. The fact that they are that distressed highlights that something is wrong, something isn't working for them, and I would urge you to do something about it. In my eyes, it isn't about you winning or losing against your dog; it isn't a competition. The aim of the game isn't to break your dog into submission; it is about a mutual respect with trusted foundations and that definitely takes time to build. It certainly won't be helped or built any quicker by refusing to give in to your dog. If you are that worried about a behaviour or you feel like you just do not know how to rectify it or how to help your dog, then reach out for tailored assistance.
- Using force will not make it better. It can be tempting to just make a dog do something, as that is how things used to be done. It is however widely accepted now that no one really learns to the best of their ability when forced to do something. Something being done under duress is not a long-term solution. It won't build those bridges of trust that we need for a long-term

relationship. If you find yourself getting wound up, upset or frustrated with your dog, try to take a step back. Easier said than done, I know. That is where a baby gate can become your best friend, as it can allow that moment for a breather when you just need a break in order to rejoin a situation and try again.

- No dog sets out to annoy you or get one over on you – I do find it laughable that people still consider this to be something that a dog spends its time doing. Dogs are far cleverer than that, so they don't waste their time on that kind of use of energy: it's much better channelled into playing, sniffing and exploring! At no point does your dog consider trying to make your life more difficult. They don't intentionally bite you to upset you – all of these behaviours happen due to other reasons that we can either learn from and move on, or keep repeating and make them far worse. It's rather like when you live with a dog who keeps running outside to bark, to patrol the fences and to check for cats or foxes. That behaviour won't have just magically appeared – it will have been days, weeks and months in the making. Starting with a puppy being encouraged for hunting in the garden, for being allowed to sit and stare and whine at every intruder into the garden, for being allowed to become over-enthusiastic about running out of the back door, creating a surge of energy, and so forth. These behaviours take time to build and 99.9 per cent of the time we have had an active role in building them.
- The dominance theory is outdated and irrelevant – although I still hear people referring to their dog as

dominant or wanting to be the alpha in the relation-ship. This theory was developed many moons ago on the basis of a dog's evolution from wolves. However, our dogs in our homes don't live with packs of other dogs; they are living in human environments, with very different dynamics from a group of wolves in the wild. A well-bred, well-rounded dog is not looking to take over your world. They certainly are not sitting on top of your sofa cushions in place of the rocks or stones they would be standing atop in the wilds outdoors, ruling over their pack. The sooner we rid ourselves of these outdated notions, the quicker we can move on and actually invest our time in learning about these incredible creatures that we share our lives with and begin using respectful techniques.

- 'My dog just . . . ' You will find everyone wanting to tell you what worked for their dog, which can at best feel helpful and at worst feel overwhelming, as their advice isn't working for your dog. That is fine, too. Don't feel bad that what you tried hasn't worked. Every dog is different, just as you are different from your mother, father, brother, sister and your partner.

- Quick fixes don't exist. As much as I'd like to be able to say otherwise, they won't work. If it's quick, it means it's not really addressing the actual issue or the reason behind it. By suppressing a behaviour, you don't simply eliminate it, it merely resurfaces in another way, in another format, and each time you suppress it, the ability to reform will become strong-er and harder to deal with, until it reaches a point where you must stop and listen. While out walking the other day, I watched a man with a Giant Schnauzer, who was on a lead in a huge park. The man kept walking the dog up to other dogs and every single time the dog was reacting – not terribly, but I wouldn't say it was going smoothly or well. The guy kept trying various things, because he was trying to suppress the behaviour as he didn't like it. He wasn't identifying which bits the dog was struggling with, or why he was reacting, which meant that the behaviour was simply going to worsen. It would most definitely become reactive and possibly end up biting a dog. That would probably be the point where the owner considers doing something about it, when he has to pay for another dog's vet bills.

- 'Don't worry, it's only playing.' Usually said when two dogs are wrestling and it feels like there is a lot of growling going on. And it's often said by the person whose dog is doing the controlling of the game! If you feel uncomfortable, or unsure, or you can tell by your dog's body language that they dislike the play, then you simply intervene and stop it. Don't feel worried about offending a stranger. You may never see them again. And if you do see them frequently, that is fine too. It is your dog and your dog's safety and confidence that are taking the hit, and it's for you to help and protect. The stranger's feelings are secondary to that.

- 'They need to learn; they could really do with being taught by another dog.' Often uttered by the owner of a puppy who has run across an entire football pitch to bowl into a dog wearing a lead and under control.

As I mentioned earlier on, this isn't something I believe in letting take place.

WHEN THE ONLY OPTION IS MEDICATION

Sometimes, the harsh reality is that a dog is struggling too much and cannot see the wood for the trees. Breeding can play a huge role in this and is something that you need to understand when selecting a puppy. Equally, the dog may need this extra help due to previous life experiences.

Often people think the main reason not to take on a puppy from a puppy farm is due to poor physical health. That is just the tip of the iceberg. The behavioural implications can be gigantic for a dog who is very badly bred, has lacked any kind of socialisation, has not been shown the world, whose mother is nervous, anxious and scared and who has been malnourished by being fed a cheap, dry food diet.

I am currently working with a client who bought a dog who was everything I've listed. The family believed the breeder when they told her the nervousness was normal, that the fear the dog was showing as a puppy was to be expected, that the intensity of the biting he was doing was to be expected. So at eight weeks, when she collected him, she believed she was getting a dog who would be everything she had dreamed a family dog could be.

Now, at five months old, we are discussing having her puppy put to sleep. His behavioural issues are so great, his biting is so bad, his ability to harm out of fear is so huge, that he could not be rehomed as he would be a threat to public safety. His owner has been hospitalised from the way he is biting her. She cannot live a life in fear of her puppy, worrying about what happens if he gets out of the baby gate. Or if a child were to look at him in the wrong way and he lunged to attack. The reality is that for some dogs, the way they were created has done too much damage. For some dogs, even medication and management won't suffice and the decision to be put to sleep has to be taken. There are a couple of rescues that have created open accommodation for dogs who do not do well living with humans, where they can exist but not meet, socialise or be with humans. While that can provide respite for those particular dogs, surely our aim should be that we are not breeding or creating these kinds of dogs.

This side of my job isn't something I share greatly on social media, as most clients are not willing to be named, to discuss it, or to share it as the upset is so huge. It certainly doesn't mean it doesn't go on, though. And please do not believe that you can escape it, if you choose to make rash decisions, not do your research or pick very unwisely all in the pursuit of a certain colour, gender or dog that looks a certain way.

There can be varying reasons why a dog may need medication to live a happy and fulfilled life. I am seeing more requiring it due to the breeding of particular dogs such as the Cockapoo.

As soon as a breed or combination of breeds starts to become popular or there is money to be made, all of the 'breeders' start crawling out of the woodwork, not caring about the actual type of dog they breed, or the implication that their breeding can have on a dog. And this is the case currently with these two breed pairings. I'm seeing frantic, anxious, hyper and fearful examples.

Sometimes the medication can be a short-term option – for example, to help with stressful periods such as fireworks, vet visits and travelling. There are many reasons why medication may also be utilised for more long-term usage such as:

- aggression towards people or other animals
- a level of anxiety that feels hard for the dog to live with
- noise fears and sensitivities
- obsessive behaviours, similar to OCD-type behaviour
- a history of trauma.

Medication is not something to be ashamed of and it certainly shouldn't be a way of judging someone and their dog. However, I do honestly feel that the lack of consideration when breeding some dogs is adding to the problems that many dogs are having. It once again reflects the ability you need to have to raise a litter of dogs that can go into a home and flourish. It certainly is not the easy task that everyone thinks it is.

Some rescue dogs who have suffered trauma or have been on the receiving end of treatment can require some low-level assistance to help rebalance them and enable them to integrate into society and lead the full and happy life that they deserve.

In order to discuss this option, you will need to find a

veterinary behaviourist – someone who is able to dispense medication to help with behaviour. This is a specialised job and something that I am not capable of doing. You should ask your own vet to refer you. It is more complicated than simply seeing your usual vet, as you really do not want to mess around with dosages and make things worse.

TAKING TABLETS

If you do have a dog who needs to be given long-term medication, along the way I've learned a few tricks which can really help your dog accept taking capsules without it becoming a wrestling match. Some dogs can be super-detectives and sniff out medication from a mile away, which is why it's often useful to teach a procedure before you actually need it. At some point in a dog's life, they are going to require medication for one thing or another.

Here are a couple of ways you can look at teaching your puppy or dog to take medicine in a kind and calm way:

1. Take something like a cocktail sausage and just feed a piece, feed another piece, feed a whole sausage, feed a whole sausage with the pill hidden in a slit cut in the side, feed a little piece of sausage straight after, feed one more piece.

   You have to get them used to a taste of something and an association of just being given it. It is worth building the association with an item like the cocktail sausage as it makes it easier for when one day you need to give the pill[s] as your dog is already accustomed to the format, the feel in their mouth and the process.

2. If your dog can be tricky about texture, i.e. the hardness of the pill inside something else, you can do a great deal of prep work beforehand. Again, you can start this with puppies, even when there are no pills to be given. First off, you need to use something hard, like a little chunk of apple, carrot or even a piece of hard kibble, and then you wrap it into another foodstuff like the sausage or a piece of cheese or something smooth like peanut butter or cream cheese. You do a few goes of feeding them the sausage with a harder object inside but not something that is offensive, so that they get used to the feeling of a harder piece within the softer food.

    Then when you actually need to give the pill, you would do the four pieces of kibble individually wrapped in a piece of cheese, give those and then give the pill wrapped in cheese and then two more pieces of kibble wrapped in cheese. Have them all ready and prepped, so you can do it in quick succession.

    If you have a Sherlock Bones dog, then make sure you wrap the pill in the sausage or foodstuff and then go and wash your hands. Then you begin the process of dispensing the food treats. This is to try to reduce the smell of cross-contamination from the pill for those detective dogs. It doesn't always work, but if you have prepared enough before using the medication pills, you stand a high chance of success.

    Do remember, though, that dogs are used to scent out the likes of cancer and other tiny molecules of disease. They aren't silly. Which is why using the association with a type of texture and food is so crucial. I've personally favoured using the cocktail sausages as Pip never gets them other times, so it feels like a real treat and he's definitely rather excited to see them appear in front of his nose.

CHAPTER TWENTY-TWO

What Your Dog Wants You to Know about Its Later Years

We all want our dogs to go on and on and on – ideally to live for ever! If only this were the case, and if only we could make it true. The best we can do for our beloved dogs is to give them the best care during their later years, to make their lives as long, happy and pain-free as possible. During a dog's senior years, physical and mental abilities obviously start to deteriorate, with the potential for illnesses such as dementia and painful ailments like arthritis, but with the right care and, sometimes, medication, we can keep a dog happy and active in its old age.

A senior dog is usually classified as such from around eight years plus. Breed, fitness levels and breeding heritage will all play a role in how fit, healthy and robust your dog remains in its later years.

The things you may start to notice in your dog as it gets older:

- Play bursts with toys on walks are not sustained; they don't go on and on. He just does a few quickfire rounds and then he shows you that's enough by going off and sniffing. Note that this won't be the case with an obsessive dog, who will continue playing through pain or discomfort.

- Hesitancy in jumping up or onto things like your bed or into the car. You may see he wants to, that he still can, but also sense a few seconds of debating it, gearing himself up to jump, and uncertainty as to whether he can manage it.
- A lack of interest in chewing harder objects. As the mouth and teeth age, you may notice differences in what your dog likes to chew on. They might not want to sit and chew on things for such a long period of time, but begin to prefer slightly softer chew options. This doesn't apply to all dogs, but it can be something to look out for if you are used to a dog who can destroy all kinds of hardcore chew objects. I would say that chewing is still important for ageing dogs, but we just need to be more mindful over what we give them.
- Some dogs in their very senior years will start to lose weight. This can be indicative of other illnesses, but some will just naturally see their appetite begin to wane as they are not as active.
- Keep an eye on their dental hygiene. Smelly breath, if it happens suddenly, can be a symptom of gastro issues. Look out for red, sore gums too. Poor dental health can cause a big impact on an elderly dog too, through making it painful to eat and creating problems internally.
- Stiffening up, taking a while to get mobile when they come out of their bed, or their back legs starting to

fail them can be indicators of a weakness or that low dosages of pain medication could be started. You should also be making their bed extremely comfortable, and position it higher off the ground so that it is easier for them to get up and it offers proper skeletal support, especially if your dog is a heavy breed.

- Barking in the night can be a common ageing issue that often gets ignored. In my experience, night barking with no obvious cause may be a symptom of possible dementia onset. It is worth discussing options with your vet as early treatment may help and there are many supplements that you can also start well before your dog becomes elderly that support brain function, etc.
- A noticeable lack of hearing or sight in certain situations that they always responded to previously, e.g. the doorbell, the cat walking into the room.

All of these are signs that you may want to slow down the activities you undertake with your dog. You wouldn't drag your eighty-year-old grandma on a Park Run, so please don't drag an older dog along on excessively long walks or runs. Understand that your dog, while still a beloved family member, may be happier with a slightly slower pace of life.

An older dog's interest in and desire for walks will change – it may want to walk less often and less far. This change should be a gradual decline rather than sharp and sudden – do visit the vet if it is the latter, as this may be a medical issue. Most older dogs, even if they can't walk as far, do still like an outing, though. With an older dog I recommend a car trip, a pootle in the garden or a visit to the beach. They will enjoy the change of scene. They just can't do as much and will need to rest much more.

I notice now that if Pip has had a particularly busy day, the next day he will want to just sleep. We don't know his exact age, but we think he's around eight years old. He is still very active, he loves to run, he loves to play, but I do see signs of slowing down, not drastic ones but tiny details that if you didn't know him, you wouldn't spot. So rather than push him to take walks every day, we take things at his pace, and give him the rest time he needs.

When it comes to exercising your older dog, please still do it! Just do it for less time and be more patient and more imaginative about what you do.

- If your dog loves water, give them a warm bath and shower and massage their joints. We used to do this with my mum's boy Barnie, as he just adored the warmth, the water and the full attention! He also loved the hairdryer, so we would do that too. It passed a good hour of time.
- Drive to quiet sniffy spots, where they can potter at their own pace and then hop back in when it's too much for them; unless you are lucky enough for your house to back on to woods.
- Take them shopping with you: less actual walking but more opportunity for sniffing and petting from people, if your dog likes people and a fuss.
- Book hydrotherapy sessions. Your insurance will often cover some of the sessions if your vet recommends them.

- If your dog is small enough, you can still take them places in your bike basket or in a dog carrier.
- Add in many more sniffing games in the garden or house. Mental stimulation will still tire your dog out, but they will also love doing something one on one with you.
- Sit on your drive or doorstep and watch the world go by together.

Most of all, we just want to make sure your dog is still doing the things it enjoys, perhaps on a lesser scale but that make its life worth living.

A NOTE ON GETTING A YOUNGER DOG AS A COMPANION

I have noticed that many dog owners, when one dog is getting older, start to consider bringing in another, younger dog, to keep the older dog buoyant and interested in life. This tends to only work if you are very careful and considerate about the dog you bring into the household. It isn't as simple as 'we love Poodles, so let's just get another one'!

Considerations to bear in mind for bringing in a new dog with an older dog:

- Your current dog's personality. Is it sociable or grumpy with other dogs? Does it enjoy playing or prefer to be alone?

- The new dog's personality. Will it be a good match or will it make the older dog's life hell?
- If you bring in a dog who is too much, too full on, too much of a bully, you could actually end up making your current dog's last years rather sad. It could make your dog withdraw from life much more quickly.
- How you will be able to manage them, separate them, train the younger one, walk the younger one alone, etc.
- How you will carve out the time to still do things with your older dog so that it doesn't feel left out?
- Who will take care of both dogs when you go away – often family and friends no longer want to help out as much when there are two dogs to look after!

Your dog's old age is when your close connection with it will pay dividends. If you have been paying attention, and you understand your dog's needs and behaviours, you will also notice when those needs and behaviours begin to change.

CHAPTER TWENTY-THREE

What Your Dog Wants You to Know about the End of Its Life

To this day I remember our black Labrador Gus lying on the kitchen floor when I was a child, for me to say goodbye to. I don't think I could really comprehend the enormity of the farewell. The experience certainly didn't prepare me for when I had to call Caroline, the home-visit vet, to come to put our darling Bulldog, Cookie, to sleep. It still makes me cry when I think about having to call her and talk about arranging the appointment, while Cookie sat at my feet panting in pain. I felt like I was betraying Cookie, even though I was making that decision based on her pain levels, based on the veterinary specialist for her heart and based on the poor-quality life she was now living. I knew it was right, I knew it was the only option left open to us, but in total honesty, it didn't feel better or easier. It felt horrific.

When I was trying to determine when the right time was to make that decision, I read everything, I researched everything, but I found it hard to pinpoint the right time to make the final decision. People kept saying things like 'You will just know', which actually isn't helpful at all. The list I've created to help you with this decision is based on my own experiences and working with clients on this hardest of choices. Even if this moment feels like a million miles away, and I hope it is for you, I recommend that you still read this section, as preparation is always better to enable you to make swifter, more informed decisions.

You really don't want to be in the position where you leave it too late and cause your dog unnecessary suffering. In every case, this is a very hard judgement to make.

For a poorly or elderly dog, these are some signs that you may need to make the decision sooner rather than later.

- Your dog has no interest in life, with no engagement in the things that they used to love – seeking out attention, playing in the garden, playing with a toy, sniffing, tottering about, chewing. A dog may continue to eat and drink, but if it has lost interest in everything else, it may be suffering.
- It feels like they are merely existing, eating, sleeping and toileting only, with nothing else happening. I so understand the feeling that you cannot bear to let them go, but in this situation it is likely that you are keeping them alive for you. Make the decision for them instead, not you.
- Your dog is panting heavily when it isn't hot and they haven't exerted themselves. This is likely to be a pain response or stress response. If the vet has already told you that your dog is reaching the end of its life, this

heavy panting is a sign that the pain or stress may be more than it can handle.

- If your dog keeps shifting positions and moving themselves, even when you have bed options that are super-comfy, it may be an indicator of physical pain for limbs like hips, back legs and knees. In this situation they won't be able to sleep or stay in one place for very long because it hurts.

- If your dog stops eating and drinking, or reduces the amount they eat. This has to be considered based on your dog's usual habits. Do bear in mind that if you have a greedy dog, it may carry on eating even if in pain or unwell, so this shouldn't be taken as a sign to continue a suffering dog's life.

- Your dog finds taking essential medication distressing. The level of medication needed to support your dog's life can also be a deciding factor. A friend recently had to make their decision based on their dog's distress at taking the medication he needed to keep him alive. The meds would only have kept him alive for a few more weeks, but the distress of getting the cocktail of drugs into him made the dog's remaining days unenjoyable, uncomfortable and distressing, so in a way, this made the decision much simpler.

- Your dog begins to suffer from incontinence, or an inability to get themselves outside to go to the loo. This can be a very hard thing for a household to live with, but in general I would say this shouldn't be a deciding factor on its own, unless your dog is in pain and is exhibiting the other signs in this list. If they are leading a happy and fulfilled life, incontinence

wouldn't be a just cause for being put to sleep. You
would need to have other contributing factors that
made you feel like this dog's life was not worth living
any longer.

- Their limbs and back end begin to give way. With
very old dogs or even some of the bigger-breed dogs,
their limbs can be the things that start to give way.
It really depends on the impact this has on them and
the pain that they have to live with, as some dogs
can manage with pain relief and physical assistance.
I'd advise you to talk the situation through with your
vet to understand at what point the pain becomes
too much. Often it is when the dosages of pain relief
stop having an impact and stop allowing the dog to
live their life.

Sadly, there are times when much younger dogs, even
puppies, have to be put to sleep, due to either a medical
reason that is no longer treatable, or due to a behavioural
reason that becomes too risky to both dogs and humans.

In my time as a behaviourist I have had to work on
cases of both and it is extremely upsetting and distressing. It never gets any easier and it is a part of the job that
isn't social media-friendly or a reality that many want to
hear. To highlight some of the behavioural reasons why a
younger dog may be put to sleep:

- Appalling breeding makes them physically and mentally so unwell that they cannot survive in this world.
- Aggression issues pose a threat to the public, endan-
gering those around them.

- A behavioural issue that has been created by a breeder which even medication cannot resolve. This could be resource guarding, it could be territorial guarding, but the only way to keep the dog alive would be for it to live out its days in a kennel environment. And for some of these dogs their love for humans can be so great that to live alone would destroy them, yet it would be unsafe for them to live with people. This is a heartbreaking decision to make, and another reason why I feel so strongly about good breeding in dogs.
- To give you an example, at a charity rehoming centre I was once working at, there was a call over the radios for a Labrador who had got out of a kennel. He ran into the food-storage room and was discovered head-deep in a kibble bag. A member of staff tried to call him, tried to lure him to no avail and so went over to put a lead on him and he turned around and savaged her arm, causing her to need surgery and be off work for weeks. The dog was only three years old and no one will ever know the experiences he had that led him to that point of distress and fear over food, but he could not legally or ethically be rehomed.
- An anxiety level that cannot be changed or reduced. This can result in the dog living a life of fear. This kind of fear will be of everything around them, of people, of noises, of going out, of doing anything but sleeping. Where sleeping becomes the only thing they are interested in and they withdraw from the world, it can be due to traumas they have seen or been a part of, especially some street dogs from abroad. This is sadly not something that can always be managed.

- If there is a level of unpredictability to a dog's behaviour that could indicate that the dog could not safely be rehomed or safely live with humans or other dogs.
- Sadly, the most common reason will be council kennels and charities having to put dogs to sleep who they know they will not be able to rehome. Or they have been abandoned on the street and the council pound cannot trace an owner, cannot find a home and have to have kennel space to take in dogs found on the streets. Many rehoming centres are overrun and simply do not have the space, so they must select the dogs that they are most likely to be able to rehome swiftly, making more room for more dogs.

The actual process of having a dog put to sleep isn't something many talk about, but I'm going to try to lay it out for you, so that you feel prepared. We sought out a wonderful palliative-care vet who assisted us and explained it all, but to help you here is my version.

If your dog is afraid of the vet, it's definitely worth paying extra to have the vet visit your home, so that your dog's last moments are spent somewhere it feels safe and comfortable. In my opinion, I'd always choose a home visit vet.

The actual process of saying a final goodbye:

1. Your sweet dog's leg fur will need to be shaved or clipped short on one of their front legs. You can do this yourself ahead of time. By the time we had Cookie put to sleep, she really was not bothered about

this. I clipped Barnie's leg as he could be feisty and I did not want to risk any chance of distress at the end.

2. A sedative can be administered, usually in the back of the neck. This ensures your dog is very calm and relaxed for the final step. Even if your dog is relaxed, you may still choose to give this sedative to ease the path and slow down their breathing. For me, as soon as this takes hold, you have said goodbye to your dog. Even now I'm sitting here sobbing, recounting this for you. It is essentially when you lose your beloved angel. They are no longer present in this world. You will find that their eyes just stare into space at this point, so be prepared for this.

3. The lethal dose is given into the leg you shaved, and your darling dog will stop breathing and die.

4. I had not considered how awful the last step would be, as you now have to either transport your dog to the pet crematorium or walk out of the vet surgery without your dog. We chose to wrap Cookie up in the softest blanket and drive her to the crematorium in Essex. It was an awful journey. I felt sick to my bones the entire way and having to take them out and leave them there just feels heartbreaking too, because it feels like you are abandoning them.

(NB When you know that you are going to have to go through this process, make sure you have your dog sitting and lying on the blanket while this procedure is carried out, so that you are then able to wrap them in the blanket from underneath and carry them to the car, paying them the respect and care that they deserve.)

Sometimes we can lose our dogs in ways we never imagined and it is impossible for me to help you prepare for those as they are so out of the blue. I know from first-hand experience, as in spring 2019 I was out walking Fred, my rescue Great Dane. We had been out for around an hour and were in the midst of playing a game. I called him and as he came running to me, he dropped to the ground. I knew he was dead the second I saw him fall. I ran to him but he was gone; there was nothing I could do. He had died immediately and, although it was hideously traumatic for me, I knew it was a good way for our beloved Fred to go.

The loss you feel when a beloved family dog dies is so huge, so gigantic and utterly heart-wrenching. In time, though, the memories of happy times will return, and you will feel grateful to know you did the best you could to give your dog not only the best life you could, but a good departure from it.

It may be due to losing three dogs within three years, but I do believe that our dogs depart our world when they feel they have taught us what we need to know.

And Finally . . .

It makes my heart sing when I see people and dogs living out their lives happily together, with mutual love and respect. That right there is my end goal for every dog I meet and work with.

The early years of life with your dog will have ups and downs; you will laugh and you will cry. I guarantee you, though, that all the hard work pays off when you see your dog settling in and becoming a part of your life. They will be your best, most loyal and most adoring friend and I hope you will be the same to them.

I truly thank you for taking the time to read this book, and to consider what your dog might want you to know. Writing the book has been a labour of love for me, and encompasses my desire to make the world a better place for these incredible creatures.

I honestly think dogs are the best things to have ever walked this planet, and I hope to have inspired you to see how much of an impact we can have on a dog's happiness and satisfaction in life.

Don't ever be scared to ask for help with your dog from

a professional such as a vet, behaviourist or other expert. We all need support networks, and dog ownership is no different.

I hope this book serves you well and perhaps one day I'll see your dog and you playing happily in the park together.

Louise
X

INDEX

ACKNOWLEDGEMENTS

People Who Need to Know
How Great They Are

When you commit to writing a book, you don't ever think you are going to be doing it during a worldwide pandemic, where there is no childcare, no school facility and where you and your husband will need to take it in turns to work. Yet that is where I find myself! I couldn't have written this without you all. So thank you . . .

To my husband, Kyle, who has caught me, lifted me and raised me up. You are truly one of a kind. I love you and I thank you for never ever saying no when I've come home with foster dogs, random dogs, cats found in a freezer . . . Nothing fazes you.

To Forest and Goldie, you being off school has been tricky to say the least! I love you with all of my heart, and you never fail to amaze me. Your love for animals shines bright and that makes me very proud.

To my mum, my dad and my sister, you are always there. Your love and enduring faith in me means the world a million times over.

ACKNOWLEDGEMENTS

To Mabel and George, my niece and nephew, for never tiring of us on FaceTime during lockdown. You kept us sane, I love you.

To my friend, Jane Kellock, for allowing me to take over your empty office during a pandemic and sit and write from it. Your generosity has allowed me to write this book.

To Pippa my publisher and her dog Bill, for meeting me at the Ace Hotel and running with the idea. And to Bill for his feedback during this process.

To Jadeen and Aimee at John Noel Management, for putting up with me, helping me and always being on the end of the phone for me. Thank you always.

To Joe Clarke at Islington Council, for all of those years ago letting me be your shadow and for believing in me.

To John Rogerson, for teaching me so much and for always being on the side of dogs. And to our time spent training in India, spurring all of us on.

To every single owner, and to every puppy and dog that I have ever come across or worked with, as you have informed me, taught me, shown me and I will be forever grateful.